# In-Class Activities Manual for Instructors of Introductory Psychology

**Patricia A. Jarvis**
*Illinois State University*

**Cynthia R. Nordstrom**
*Illinois State University*

**Karen B. Williams**
*Illinois State University*

Boston    Burr Ridge, IL    Dubuque, IA    Madison, WI    New York    San Francisco    St. Louis
Bangkok    Bogotá    Caracas    Kuala Lumpur    Lisbon    London    Madrid    Mexico City
Milan    Montreal    New Delhi    Santiago    Seoul    Singapore    Sydney    Taipei    Toronto

## McGraw-Hill Higher Education

A Division of The McGraw-Hill Companies

IN-CLASS ACTIVITIES MANUAL FOR INSTRUCTORS OF
INTRODUCTORY PSYCHOLOGY
PATRICIA A. JARVIS, CYNTHIA R. NORDSTROM, AND KAREN B. WILLIAMS

This book is printed on acid-free paper.

4 5 6 7 8 9 0 QPD QPD 0 3 2

ISBN 0-07-238431-X

www.mhhe.com

# Table of Contents

# Acknowledgments

This activity manual was conceived as a support supplement for instructors of large sections of Introductory Psychology courses. We have included activities we have developed and ones we have gleaned from sources over many years of teaching in the "trenches" and adapted for use in large sections. After many hallway conversations on what we did in class that "worked", we decided to compile the activities that we use for others to use. We each typically teach sections of approximately 200-300 students and have found time and again that these activities engage students in large sections with the material in a way that enhances their appreciation and understanding of our field.

Some of the sources for some of our material are missing. As the nature of using activities like the ones in this manual involves a hand-me-down approach across instructors and instructor's manuals, we were not able to identify every individual who may be the author of some of the activities given herein. We have made extensive efforts to locate the authors and copyright owners of each of the activities we ourselves did not create, and we hope that appropriate credit has been cited for those activities. However, if we have not given proper credit, we would appreciate hearing from anyone with such knowledge at pajarvis@ilstu.edu. We apologize for any oversights in this regard. We gratefully acknowledge those individuals who granted us permission to adapt their activities for this manual.

We most gratefully acknowledge the multitude of students at Illinois State University, who have encouraged us to try new teaching methods and have reminded us that their learning needs were as important as our teaching needs. We also gratefully acknowledge Joseph Terry, Senior Editor at McGraw-Hill and Don Mason, Sales Representative, for supporting us on this project. We also appreciate the help of Fred Spears, Susan Kunchandy, and Barbara Santoro, Assistant Editors at McGraw-Hill. We also are indebted to Kathryn Anderson and Suzanne Ferrara in our department for their very capable help and assistance in typing and editing this manual. A thank you is also extended to our colleague, Macon Williams, for helping us locate source material. We give a special "thank you" to Heidi Ostergaard, Leatrice Brooks, Cory Baxter, Melissa Curran, Juli Sabelka, Kim Starkweather, and Matt Cain for locating source material and proofreading the manual. Each of us also thank the significant others in our lives who support and encourage us every day.

P. A. J.
C. R. N.
K. B. W.

# Chapter 1

# Introduction

**'And yet the true creator is necessity, which is
the mother of invention.' -- Plato**

Like many projects, this activity manual was borne out of pure frustration. All three of the authors routinely teach large sections of introductory psychology ($N > 300$). Similar to most educators, we are constantly trying to find new and better ways of reaching our students. We are ever mindful that students' first experiences with psychology will likely determine: (a) their view of our field and (b) whether we subsequently see them in more advanced psychology classes.

However, through experience we know that being able to really connect with students is difficult in a large classroom. Many of the ways of connecting with students that serve us well in a small class are virtually impossible in a large class (e.g., learning all students' names, having debates, conducting experiments, etc.) (Carbone, 1998). Compounding the problem is that most of the ancillary materials for introductory psychology classes (computer applications, transparency masters, instructor's manuals) are targeted toward small or moderately sized classes. For those of us who teach large classes, this can be extremely frustrating. Our colleagues in psychology have generated a variety of very useful ideas to help students understand psychological concepts, but many of these ideas as represented in instructor's manuals are impossible to use given the constraints of a large class. For example, activities may involve distributing multiple handouts, asking students to leave class and make behavioral observations, or requiring students to work in small groups. Those of us who teach large sections know that just distributing a single handout can take ten minutes of class time!

Thus, those of us who teach large classes find ourselves in a bit of a conundrum. We want to reach our students and know that many of the classroom activities that others have developed are a way to achieve this but find most activity manuals difficult to use in a large class. Our solution has been threefold. First, over the years we have created and refined our own classroom activities. Second, we have adapted others' ideas to make them more amenable to a large classroom environment. Third, we have met continuously to swap ideas about those activities that work and those that do not.

During the course of our discussions, we found ourselves repeating, "Wouldn't it be nice if we didn't have to spend our time trying to reconfigure small class materials so that they would work in large sections?" The net result is this activity manual designed

1

specifically to address the challenges of teaching large section introductory psychology courses. From a philosophical standpoint, the activities are based upon the premise that when students are actively engaged with the material, they will learn more (i.e., active learning). From a practical standpoint, the activities are designed to be brief and easy to use but nonetheless have impact. Additionally, we have included a number of other materials that the instructor responsible for a large section may find helpful (e.g., a sample syllabus, teaching tips, recommendations for effectively using graduate assistant resources, etc.). We hope that others "in the trenches" of large section psychology classes will find this manual helpful.

**What is active learning and what makes it an effective teaching tool?**

Since this activity manual is designed to promote active learning in large classes, an obvious question is, "What is active learning"? An active learning environment is achieved when students are involved in more than simply listening to information; instead, they are actively engaged with the information (Modell & Michael, 1993). In an active learning situation, the role of the instructor is to assist the student in building his or her own personal understanding of the material. Thus, the emphasis is not on the instructor imparting information (i.e., as in the case in a traditional lecture format) but rather on the student actively working with the information. Students are using their brains . . . solving problems, examining information, applying ideas and concepts. In short, active learning requires the student to think about the information, not just record the information.

There are many different classroom techniques that have been suggested as means of promoting active learning. Some of these techniques include: debates, discussion groups, demonstrations, role-plays, mini-experiments, polling, fishbowl, games, etc. What all of these techniques share in common is that they are a departure from the typical lecture format in which students passively take in information.

From a pedagogical standpoint, active learning offers several distinct student advantages including better retention, better retrieval, and in general a better ability to use the acquired information in different contexts (Modell & Michael, 1993). But while the benefits of active learning are well known (Modell & Michael, 1993), many instructors mistakenly believe that such a philosophy cannot be applied to a large lecture hall setting (i.e., in classes with more than 50 students). We believe that not only can active learning be used in large section classes, it is imperative to do so. Students in large section classes may be more prone to disengage and tune out of what is going on in class relative to smaller classes. When students disengage it is not improbable to expect that their attendance and consequent class performance will suffer. Moreover, from a purely pragmatic viewpoint, larger classes now seem to be normative in both small colleges as well as universities. Benjamin (1991) reports that the average undergraduate class size has increased over the past several years. Given these realities, adapting active learning principles for use in the larger classroom makes sense.

**Are there other benefits associated with active learning?**

In a word, Yes! Aside from the pedagogical benefits, active learning also yields a number of other positive outcomes.

■ **Active Learning Creates Social Opportunities.**

Due to the nature of many of the exercises incorporated in this manual, students have the opportunity to connect with one another in meaningful ways in a classroom setting. Students have the chance to talk with one another, share ideas, argue constructively, etc. The classroom now serves not just an educational function but a social function as well.

The social aspects of active learning in large introductory psychology courses are quite evident. The majority of students enrolled in the course are freshmen. It is not uncommon for many students to report that there are more students in their introductory psychology class than in the entire senior body of the high school they attended? It also is quite common for students to report that most of their initial course work takes place in large lecture halls. For a student trying to make the adjustment from high school to college, this type of classroom scenario does little to help them build relationships. Active learning in the classroom can help students to feel less isolated. Moreover, students who have grown accustomed to interacting with one another will feel more comfortable asking questions in a large lecture hall.

■**Active Learning Provides for Different Learning Styles.**

Most instructors recognize that there are many different types of learners. Silberman (1996) notes that there are at least three major types of learners. Some learners learn best by observing others. These "visual" students prefer carefully organized lectures and seem content to write down what the instructor tells them. Other students might be described as "auditory" learners in that they learn best by listening to information rather than taking careful notes. Finally, "kinesthetic" learners prefer active involvement with the material. Rather than watching and listening, these students like to "do." The traditional lecture format tends to be targeted toward the first type of learner and may leave some students struggling. Active learning, on the other hand, has something to offer all three types of learners with its emphasis on visual, auditory, and hands-on experiences.

It also is fair to say that relatively few students are exclusively one type of learner. Many students learn best when a combination of modalities is used to present the material. Thus, teaching should incorporate multiple sensory channels. This recommendation is consistent with research by Schroeder (1993), which suggests that 60% of incoming college students tend to have a practical as opposed to a theoretical approach to learning. Students appear to prefer concrete, practical learning experiences rather than abstract, reflective experiences. Silberman (1996) points out that such an orientation to learning is perhaps not surprising given the kind of world in which students live (sound bites, fast-paced presentation of information, MTV, etc.).

**Why might an instructor resist using active learning techniques?**

There are a variety of reasons an instructor might be resistant to the idea of using active learning in his/her classroom. Some of the common concerns we have heard voiced include the following:

- **Active Learning Eats Up Too Much Class Time.**

Many instructors feel compelled to cover a finite amount of material in a course. It is as if instructors are competing for a prize that can be won only if they finish "x" number of chapters, use "x" number of overheads, etc. We humbly suggest that this is the wrong orientation. While there is little doubt that the lecture presents an efficient way to present a lot of material, one might question how much students really learn and take away with them. An active learning classroom will typically cover less material but in deeper more meaningful ways. As psychologists, we know that when students process information at a deeper level, they are more likely to retain and use the information at a later date.

- **Active Learning Requires Too Much Preparation
Time on the Part of Instructors.**

While it is true that active learning does require additional preparation time, we consider this a worthwhile trade off given the outcomes (i.e., effective learning, class interest, etc.). Moreover, we have deliberately fashioned the activities in the manual to cut down on instructor's up-front preparation time. Some of the features we incorporated to minimize preparation time include:

- **Perforation**
  The manual has been perforated so that instructors can tear out relevant activities and bring them directly to class.
- **Font Size**
  A larger font size has been used for each activity to facilitate use of activities as printed in class.
- **Instructions**
  We have used a simple step-by-step description for each activity so that instructors can easily follow along.
- **Transparencies**
  Prepared pages for relevant activities are included and can be xeroxed and easily made into overhead transparencies.
- **Choice of Activities**
  We have also included a number of different activities per chapter so that instructors can pick and choose depending on the material they wish to cover, the time they have available, and their level of comfort with a given activity.

A final note on preparation time—like most aspects of working in academia (delivering lectures, preparing a manuscript for publication, etc.), the more practice one has with the task, the less preparation required. We suspect that after instructors have successfully used an activity multiple times, the activity will become as natural to a given block of material as the instructor's lecture notes, thereby minimizing preparatory time.

### ■ Active Learning is Nothing More Than "Fun and Games."

In response to the assertion that active learning is nothing more than fun and games, we would point to the research described earlier, which supports active learning from a pedagogical standpoint. We would also point out that there is nothing wrong with promoting the notion that learning can and should be fun. Is there anything worse than when students shuffle into a lecture hall, and plop down in their desks with a long-suffering look on their faces that seems to shout, "How much longer before class is over?" Although this is anecdotal evidence, we routinely find that students are not constantly checking their watches, or packing up their materials ten minutes before the end of class when an active learning environment was created in class. Perhaps more telling . . . students actually seem to be smiling (yes, smiling!) when they leave class (and we suspect it is not just because class is over!). Does such a reaction make it more likely that students will return for the next class? We suspect that it does. Given such an experience, are instructors more likely to look forward to the next class period? Again, we believe this to be the case.

### ■ Students Are Unaccustomed to Active Learning and Will Resist It.

We cannot really disagree with this argument. It *is* the case that students typically are unused to active learning and therefore may seem wary of it at first. Oftentimes students are accustomed to being passive learners with little more to do in class than take notes. Some students (and instructors!) have the erroneous belief that the only useful information comes out of the mouth of the instructor. Students may view active learning as a waste of class time. However, we find that students who seemed a tad uneasy about active learning at first come around to it over time. This is particularly the case when active learning is introduced gradually and it is used to complement (as opposed to replace) a well organized lecture.

**Related Readings:**

Benjamin, L. T. (1991). Personalization and active learning in the large introductory psychology class. *Teaching of Psychology*, **18**, 68–74.

Carbone, E. (1998). **Teaching large classes: Tools and strategies**. Thousand Oaks, CA: Sage Publications, Inc.

Modell, H. I., and Michael, J. A. (Eds.), (1993). **Promoting active learning in the life science classroom.** New York: New York Academy of Sciences.

Silberman, M. (1996). **Active learning: 101 strategies to teach any subject.** Needham Heights, MA: Allyn and Bacon.

# Chapter 2

# Some Lessons from the Trenches

1. Make the subject matter impact upon your students, personally and collectively.

2. The teacher should not be reluctant to show weaknesses. Always be honest and sincere.

3. Personalize the subject matter. Remind students on the first day that the course is really about them.

4. Make students want to come to class each day. Forecast tomorrow.

5. Enjoy each class daily and let students know that you do by showing it (laugh, praise, challenge). Allow yourself to be "young" some of the time.

6. **Be human.** They will love it and rally to you. Emote when appropriate.

7. Tell them they are all "A students" until they prove otherwise (many will, early on).

8. Always keep abreast of where you (they) are in the course. Inform students regularly about "coming events."

9. Always inform students well in advance of tests, and due dates for projects, papers, etc.

10. Always be enthusiastic. If students know you enjoy your work and the subject matter, they have a tendency to do the same.

11. Challenge students on tests. Expect them to do well. They will try to fulfill your prophecies.

12. Try to parallel subject matter to the present and to students' worlds, needs, failures, and successes.

13. Draw out every student. Make every student feel important. Let them know that you feel this way about them.

14. Be a good listener. Turn on all the "perceptive switches" when you walk through the classroom door. You will be amazed what you will see and hear. That class is alive every day.

15. **Relate, relate, relate,** but never try to "cross over." You are an adult with years of experiences, and they are young people.

16. Utilize outside speakers and movies. Movies should be current, and speakers' topics must be pertinent. Commercial TV is a tough competitor and can make even some of the better classroom movies seem mundane to students.

17. The best answer to anger is sometimes silence. The best answer to inappropriate behavior is to ignore it or be silent in the face of it. Attention to it is a reinforcer. It will usually extinguish itself.

Compiled by Paul Rosenfeld. Reprinted in the Instructor's Manual to accompany Feldman's **Understanding Psychology** (4th Edition) written by Todd Zakrajsek.

## Tips For Effective Management of Large Sections

**(Adapted from Whitford, 1996)**

### Sections Over 100 Students

One aspect of the large class that is often overlooked is that students, as a rule, do not like to sit through lectures. A student's interest level is usually the class period minus 10 minutes. This aspect seems to be a universal constant. Try to use in-class activities, guest speakers, films, videos, and demonstrations as much as possible to augment and break up your lectures. Keep student interest high and, thus, attendance at a maximum. A most disappointing event is to come to a large class and see only about 30% of the class in attendance. You should strive to have all your students so happy with the class that they want to attend every period.

## In-Class Activities in Large Sections

Brief activities can enhance your lectures and student enthusiasm for your course. Even though activities are challenging in a large class, you should try a few during your first term; this will give you a feel for the type of problems that you are likely to confront in future activities.

## Videos in Large Sections

Videos can be very up-to-date and interesting. However, a major drawback to videos is that many schools do not have large format projection video players, but rather TVs and VCRs. These have limited use because of the size of the screen, thus the number of students who can view the programming is limited. A possibility is to show videos outside of the regular class time. Plan to have a smaller room and show the video several times each day. If you wish, you could keep roll or have questions on your examination. Improved technical innovations have occurred within the last five years lowering the cost of video projectors to below the range of $3,000. If you can obtain the funding for a video projector system, it will greatly enhance your ability to show videos to large classes.

## Handouts in Large Sections

Handouts for large classes can be expensive to produce for the quantity necessary, but they are useful. Handouts can be worthwhile and students like them. Disadvantages of handouts are the costs of production, your time assembling the information, and the problem of students who miss class and want a copy of the handout from a week ago. You will find yourself either carrying a pile of old handouts or having a line of students trailing you back to your office. A possible solution to the handout problem is to include them in the syllabus or sell the students these overheads at your cost through your bookstore. It also can be disadvantageous to use handouts in a large section due to the time it takes to hand them out. Ask students to volunteer to help distribute handouts and this becomes less problematic.

## Specific Problems of Large Sections

Classes of over 100 students have the additional problem of background noise. Very large classes can drown out your voice in the back of the room. Many students in the back of the room may simply lose interest because they cannot hear you; use the microphone when available. Students' talking in large classes also disrupts the class and annoys the instructor. Be specific and forceful about this the first time it happens. One method that works is to not enter the room until you are ready to lecture and the class period has just begun. Try to enter from the front of the room near the podium, open your notes, and start to lecture. If you are consistent with your arrival time, students will become accustomed to this method and will settle down more rapidly. Realize that if you lose control (students talking, rustling papers, reading the newspaper) of a very large class, it is hard to regain control in that class period. Finally, ask students for their attention and when they quiet down thank them for doing so.

## Learning Student Names in Large Sections

Learning the names of students in large classes is almost impossible. You might try to learn the names of a few students around the room and use them whenever possible to communicate to students that you are at least attempting to learn who they are. Also, have students who volunteer for demonstrations, etc., introduce themselves to the class. Use their names during that lecture whenever possible.

## When Things Go Wrong

No matter how hard you try to set up your class, there will be occasions when things will go wrong. Stay as flexible as you can and adopt the attitude that these mishaps can be turned into a positive means of improving your course. Specifically, avoid letting a student publicly engage you in a personal discussion about a grade or a course policy. You do not give grades, rather students earn their grades, and the course policies apply equally to everyone in the course. The next time you teach the course, it will be much easier; the major mistakes will have been corrected. Additionally, you will be less nervous the more you teach, although you will always be a little nervous (especially in the large classes). Adopt the attitude that this is your best effort and improvements are sure to follow.

## Things to Consider When Structuring Your Large Section

The following are some suggestions about how to maximize the impact of your presentations when designing your class.

1. COME TO CLASS PREPARED. Do not let the class flow without structure. Have a lecture planned and stick to it. The use of learning points is a good method to give structure to the class.

2. ALWAYS START THE CLASS ON TIME. If you are late, the students will learn when class really starts and they will start to come to class later and later. Make the first several minutes very important; talk about the next examination and give specific details about projects. Make the material relevant to the text and test so that students who are ready and taking notes will be rewarded. Then, use a lecture launcher to grab attention. Many of the activities in this manual are designed so that they may be used in this way.

3. TRY TO AVOID OPEN-ENDED PHILOSOPHICAL QUESTIONS. The students typically do not care about the meaning of life, animal rights, or ethical applications of psychological principles. In smaller upper-division classes, these types of questions

can be very productive. Ask questions that do not require a large amount of background knowledge. Many introductory students will not have the necessary background to answer very complex questions.

4. **RESPECT STUDENTS.** You have finally achieved some status in your academic area, but do not try to reduce your frustrations with other faculty members during your graduate career by showing disrespect for your students. Remember, they are you several years earlier.

5. **ESTABLISH THAT YOU ARE IN CHARGE OF THE CLASS.** Do not let students talk or be disruptive in class. Occasionally, there will be a student who asks questions that seem inappropriate to the main thrust of the class. If this student persists, ask the student to save his or her question for after the class. Students have little difficulty getting their instructor off track and onto a tangent. Most students can figure out that this tangential material will not be on the examination, and some students will try to direct your attention from the lecture.

6. **USE TERMINOLOGY THAT IS APPROPRIATE FOR A STUDENT'S LEVEL.** Be mindful of your language both in your lectures and in examinations. When 50% of the class asks the meaning of a specific term on an examination, you know that the level is inappropriate.

7. **WHEN WRITING YOUR EXAMINATIONS, BE AS SPECIFIC AS POSSIBLE.** Make the questions easier than you think they need to be. You have just learned the material at a level the instructor must master, not at the level of an entering freshman.

8. **DO NOT WRITE TRICKY QUESTIONS ON EXAMINATIONS.** If a student knows the material, he or she wants to receive credit for a correct answer. Do not be obscure in your wording or syntax.

9. **BE SURE TO COVER MATERIAL EMPHASIZED ON EXAMINATIONS.** As you teach the class, you will learn how much material you can cover in a specific time period. Students will complain if you ask exam questions on material not covered. You can always start the first lecture after an examination, but be sure that you tell the students where the material for the current examination ends.

10. **MINIMIZE THE TURNAROUND TIME FOR TEST GRADING.** Since you are more likely to use multiple choice tests in large sections, try to have them scored as soon as possible. You might consider including a last page to your exam with blanks for students to complete after they finish the exam. They may tear this off the exam and take it with them. Then, post the answers to the test so they may check their answers within an hour of the end of the exam. Students appreciate immediate reinforcement. Consider using three forms of an exam with questions (and/or answers) scrambled across forms. Distribute forms in stacks from the front of the lecture hall to the rear. Distribute a stack of Form A, followed by a stack of Form B, and finally Form C. Students have more difficulty seeing over the head of someone directly in front of

them (who has the same form of the test) than someone on either side who has a different form of the exam. This reduces cheating.

11. **ENCOURAGE STUDENTS TO CHALLENGE ANY EXAM QUESTIONS** they do not understand or think they answered correctly in writing.

12. **ENCOURAGE STUDENTS TO CHECK THEIR ANSWERS** against the key and their posted score. If there are discrepancies, encourage the students to meet with you or your teaching assistants.

13. **ASK THE STUDENTS TO EITHER WRITE DOWN AREAS OF THE LECTURE THAT THEY DO NOT UNDERSTAND** or to meet with you or the teaching assistants to discuss areas that are not clearly understood.

14. **ENCOURAGE NONTRADITIONAL STUDENTS.** These can be students over traditional age, foreign students, English as a Second Language students, individuals with special needs, and persons with both physical and learning disabilities. Take the time to accommodate these students and encourage them as much as possible.

## Selecting the Type of Questions

With large classes, you almost surely will use some form of multiple choice or objective computer-scored examinations. During the planning phase of your course, determine the types of statistics you can expect to get with your examination scores from the computer-based scoring system. These statistics will vary from school to school, but get as much data as you can with each examination. If your school can produce bi-serial $r$ statistics, they can be useful in evaluating your own test items.

## Cheating in a Large Section

Cheating can be a problem in the large class. Round up four or five TAs and ask them to help proctor the examination. At the beginning of the examination give the students a short "do not cheat" lecture intended to let them know what to expect if you catch them cheating. The sheer mass of the TAs present will stop most cheating. Using multiple forms of the exam with the questions arranged in different orders also serves as a good safeguard against cheating.

## Related Reading:

Whitford, F. (1996). **Teaching psychology** (2nd ed.). A guide for the new instructor. Englewood Cliffs, NJ: Prentice-Hall.

Anyone who has taught a large section of introductory psychology will agree that a good teaching assistant is a highly valued asset. A teaching assistant can play a vital role in the success of a class (Carbone, 1998; Wulff, Nyquist, & Abbott, 1987). The following guidelines may help you in obtaining, selecting, training, and managing this valuable resource.

**Recruiting and Selecting A Teaching Assistant**

■ **Obtaining a Good Teaching Assistant**

Most departments assign graduate teaching assistants to faculty teaching large lecture sections of introductory psychology. However, if your department is unable to make this assignment, it may be possible to recruit upper-level undergraduate assistants to help with your course. You may approach previous students from your classes. Current assistants often make excellent referrals for future assistants. Students will be more attracted to the position if they see the opportunities that assisting can give to them. It is important that students realize that their experiences can be as valuable as their tuition waivers or stipends. Make it clear that TAs can learn important skills that will make them more competitive in the job market (e.g., oral communication, managing, coaching, etc.). For students interested in an educational career, the assistantship serves as a wonderful mentoring opportunity.

■ **What to Look for in Choosing Your Assistant**

When making a selection decision, consider what you may want your teaching assistant to do. The roles of teaching assistants vary greatly. For instance, tasks may include grading, recording grades, proctoring exams, holding office hours, tutoring, helping with demonstrations, giving guest lectures, attending class, and taking notes.

Select an assistant who demonstrates the knowledge and abilities necessary to carry out the tasks most important to you. For example, grading and recording grades requires attention to detail, organization, and integrity. Holding office hours and tutoring requires good verbal communication, interpersonal skills, diagnostic ability, and leadership. Presenting information to the class requires energy, professionalism, verbal communication, and impact.

**Training and Developing a Teaching Assistant**

- **Training a Teaching Assistant**

Most jobs require some level of training. The same is true for the position of teaching assistant. Do not assume that your assistant will intuitively know what you expect. Be clear in your expectations!

Preparing a job description for assistants has helped us. We have included one for you to use or edit as you like (**see Example 2.1**). Include a brief description of all major duties you expect your teaching assistant to perform. Go over these duties with your assistant and provide your assistant a copy of the job description and the course syllabus prior to the class. Clarify all expectations up front. How often do you expect the TA to hold office hours? What are your policies about missing office hours? Will the TA be expected to attend all classes? When will the TA post grades?, etc.

Schedule an orientation session with your TA(s). Be very specific about how you want duties carried out. For example, be clear in how you want students to proctor. Clarify where and when the student should show up to proctor. Explain what you expect the TA to do—help pass out exams, walk around the room, answer questions, etc. Make sure you explain what the TA should do in the event of someone cheating. Give your TA authority when dealing with students and suggestions for how to handle students who question such authority. Introduce your TA to the class and make it clear that you expect them to treat the TA with the same respect they give you. If you disagree with a TA, do this in private—not in front of a student. Come to a mutually acceptable agreement with the TA before informing the student how the situation will be handled. Asking the teaching assistant what concerns they have about the course is useful at the beginning of the course as well as throughout the semester.

Because teaching assistants are both teachers and students, the boundary between these two roles often is blurred. Many TAs struggle with dual relationship problem. Since they are put in a position of authority over peers, you might want to discuss how they should handle this responsibility. APA provides some guidelines on dual relationships you might refer to as well. Preparing a TA to handle situations, such as those described above, in advance can greatly reduce potential problems in the future.

- **Developing a Teaching Assistant**

Being a teaching assistant can be a wonderful learning opportunity for students. In particular, assisting a professor in teaching a course can be an extremely useful experience for graduate students going on to academic positions. Recall the first time you presented a lecture. Most of us can admit to being scared and nervous. Encourage your assistant to present part of a lecture or conduct one or more of the activities in this manual with the class. Help with preparation. Provide useful tips (e.g., use overheads, give multiple examples, speak slowly, etc.). Give the TA constructive feedback. In larger sections, most teaching assistants are very unsure about presenting in front of such a large group. You must judge whether your TA can handle this or not and you most likely will want to save this for near the end of the course (after Teaching Evaluations).

Many of our assistants' interpersonal skills improve as a function of working with students. Freshman students offer many opportunities to practice patience, dispute resolution skills, and discipline. Encourage your TA to share any problems he or she is having and talk through ways to approach and manage the problem.

Many universities offer teaching workshops for faculty and graduate assistants. Make teaching assistants aware of these opportunities. For example, many of our graduate teaching assistants recently attended a seminar (Lessons from the Trenches) offered by our University's Center for the Advancement of Teaching. The workshop offered teaching suggestions from several "seasoned" faculty members. Students appreciated the opportunity and felt they had learned some valuable information. In addition, our center offers workshops in developing Teaching Portfolios, which are very helpful for students planning to seek employment in academic settings.

**Managing Your Teaching Assistant**

Setting and communicating expectations clearly and early with our TAs alleviates most potential problems. However, we do have an occasional TA who is late for office hours, delays posting exams, skips out on proctoring, etc. When a problem arises, discuss it with the TA immediately. Discuss how to avoid the problem in the future and discuss consequences if the behavior continues in the future. Make sure to document these conversations if they should occur.

Appraise your TA's performance and give constructive feedback. Make sure you point out both positive and negative aspects of performance. Suggest ways the TA can improve. Put your recommendations in writing so that the teaching assistant may review them from time to time and include them in their teaching portfolio. Show your appreciation for a job well done. Our department presents awards for good TA performance. These monetary awards provide an extra incentive to work hard and improve skills. It also is important that you monitor the demands you place on your assistant. Respect their time and do not expect them to devote more than their allotted hours to you.

Hopefully the suggestions we have offered will be useful to you as you work with student assistants. We encourage you to communicate with your assistants regularly giving them an opportunity to get to know you as a colleague in this special out-of-classroom learning experience.

**Related Readings:**

Carbone, E. (1998). **Teaching large classes: Tools and strategies.** Thousand Oaks, CA: Sage Publications, Inc.

Modell, H. I., and Michael, J. A. (Eds.), (1993). **Promoting active learning in the life science classroom.** New York: New York Academy of Sciences.

Nyquist, J. D., Wulff, D. H., and Abbott, R. D. (1997). Students' perceptions of large classes. In M. Weimer (Ed.), **New directions for teaching and learning: Teaching large classes well** (pages 17–30). San Francisco: Jossey-Bass.

Whitford, F. (1996). **Teaching psychology** (2nd Edition). A guide for the new instructor. Englewood Cliffs: Prentice-Hall.

Zakrajsek, T. (1997). **Instructor's Manual to Accompany Feldman's Understanding Psychology** (4th Edition). Boston: McGraw-Hill, Inc.

Example 2.1

## Teaching Assistant Job Description

### Job Summary

Attends class and assists instructor with classroom activities; occasionally lectures to the class or discussion groups; proctors and grades exams; performs routine clerical tasks; holds regular office hours and answers students' questions; provides individual instruction; keeps instructor informed of any problems; follows the APA ethics guidelines.

### Job Duties

1. Attends class and assists instructor by taking notes on the lecture material, distributing handouts, performing classroom demonstrations, running audiovisual equipment, and proctoring exams.
2. Prepares and presents guest lectures to the class, organizes and facilitates study or discussion groups.
3. Grades computer-scored exams and written assignments. Provides instructor with grade summary report and item statistics.
4. Performs routine clerical tasks such as photocopying, recording grades, filing exams and other assignments, keeping track of attendance records, posting exams scores, etc.
5. Holds regular office hours and schedules appointments with students.
6. Answers students' questions or directs students to appropriate parties. Reviews exams with students, provides individual instruction and tips for study management. Refers student to instructor and keeps instructor informed of progress of any problems. Always follows the APA ethics guidelines when working with students.

### *Important Knowledge, Skills, and Abilities*
- Attention to detail
- Organization and Information Retrieval
- Integrity
- Good Verbal Ability and Interpersonal Skills
- Analytical and Diagnostic Ability
- Leadership
- Professionalism
- Initiative and Motivation

# Chapter 3

# Sample Syllabus

---

**GENERAL PSYCHOLOGY**
Class meets in _____
on Mondays, Wednesdays, and Fridays
from 9:00 to 9:50

Fall, 1999

## COURSE SYLLABUS

---

This course surveys the field of psychology. You will learn that psychologists have concerns that range from determining the smallest amount of light energy you can detect to understanding the causes of mental illness. But whether they are interested in basic research or applying knowledge, all psychologists acknowledge a debt to the scientific method. Throughout this course you will learn how the scientific method has been employed in the study of behavior in addition to the many ways psychological methods and knowledge have been applied to helping people.

## Instructor

Patricia A. Jarvis, Ph.D.
Professor
425 DeGarmo Hall (Office)
(309) 438–8425 (leave message and number, if I am not available)
Office Hours: Mon & Wed 10:00 to 10:50 and 1:15 to 2:00 (or by appointment)

## Text

The following text is required and is available at both the Alamo and the Bone Student Center Bookstores:

**Feldman, R. (1999). Understanding Psychology (5th ed.). New York: McGraw-Hill.**

If you would like to purchase a Study Guide that goes with your text, ask for one at the bookstore or let me know and I will make sure one is ordered for you. This is not required, but may be helpful to you **if you use it**.

## Graduate Teaching Assistants

Given the large size of the class (approximately 330 students), it would be impossible for one individual to deal with so many students. Thus, the Psychology department has assigned two Graduate Teaching Assistants (TAs) to this class. If your last name begins with any letter from **A–M,** your TA will be _____ and if your last name begins with any letter from **N–Z,** your TA will be _____. Thus, direct your questions to your TA. They will announce their office hours the first week of classes. These individuals are extremely dedicated and capable of helping you succeed in this course. They can be found during their office hours at desk # 22B **outside** of your instructor's office (Room 425 DeGarmo Hall). They will attend class and take notes in order to help you with your questions about the course material. However, you will not have access to their notes. You must attend class and take your own notes. If you miss class, you are responsible for anything you missed and you will have to get notes from another classmate if you can find one who will help you. You are expected to treat your Graduate Teaching Assistants with the same respect you give your instructor.

You are responsible for knowing your grade in the course at all times. The TAs will keep records on the grades and will be available for you to meet with them and go over your tests after you take them. Thus, any questions about the course material and your grades must be directed to them. If you are not satisfied with their answers, then please see me during my office hours or by appointment.

## Attendance

You are required to attend all class meetings **on time and for the entire time.** Lectures are designed to improve your understanding of the material in the text, as well as to supplement it. A substantial number of exam questions will be drawn directly from these lectures.

## Professor-Student Expectations

In teaching this course, I am highly motivated to teach as creatively and energetically as possible. In addition, I strive to be fair and reasonable, and to treat each of you with respect. I agree to come to every class, on time, prepared with thoughtful, relevant, and up-to-date material.

By enrolling in this class you agree that you plan to come to every class, on time, having completed all assigned work, prepared to think, listen, question, and participate. You agree to treat me, the Graduate Teaching Assistants, each other, the classroom setting, and the educational process with dignity and respect. You agree to seriously commit yourselves to engaging in the level of work that this course demands.

Consequences resulting from your failure to meet my expectations of you in this course may include, but are not limited to, asking you to leave the class for one class period and meet with me before you return to the next class meeting, assigning you a seat in the class, or referring you to the Student Judicial Office for misconduct.

As our class is quite large, you may expect to be a passive learner, yet there is ample research supporting that active participation in learning enhances retention of material. To foster your active participation, there will be a number of in-class activities designed to engage you actively with the material. It is expected that you will take advantage of these opportunities by volunteering when asked to do so and/or actively attending to the material presented.

I have found in ten years of teaching this course that some students find the pace of the lectures to be a bit fast for their processing abilities. This is especially so in large lecture hall sections. If this is true for you, you may find that having read the assigned reading before coming to class enhances your lecture processing speed. You also might try to listen and write only the main points of the lecture. It is impossible to write everything I say. Finally, you are welcome to record my lectures as long as you operate your equipment. You may also ask me to repeat key points or simply slow down as necessary, and I will be happy to do so.

**Examinations**

There will be **five** exams during the semester. Their dates are given on the assignment sheet attached at the end of this syllabus. The exams will contain 60 multiple-choice questions covering the material (text and lectures) presented since the previous exam. During finals week, there will be an optional cumulative, 100 question final exam on which material previously tested will have equal representation. Thus, there will be a total of six exams in this course. There will be no make-up exams, but you may drop your lowest exam grade and replace it with the final. If you choose to take the final, it must be taken **at the time it is scheduled**. Your final grade will thus be based on your five highest exam grades. If you take the final and perform more poorly on it than your lowest semester exam grade, the final exam will not be counted.

You may take an exam early if you must miss class for a University-sponsored event (such as band, debate, or your position on a sports team) if you make arrangements with me one week prior to taking the exam. If you know or suspect that you have a learning disability, test anxiety, etc., you may arrange to take your exams through Disability Concerns. I recommend this, but you must arrange it with them and let me know a week in advance of each exam that you will be taking your exams in Fell Hall so that I can make sure an exam will be there for you.

**Grading**

Each of the exams will be worth 60 points and the quiz will be worth 40 points for a total of 340 for five required exams (remember you may drop the lowest of the five exams and replace it with the optional final exam resulting in four exams plus the final). On each exam the following grading scale applies: 54–60 = A, 48–53 = B, 42–47 = C, 36–41 = D, and below 36 = F. Your final grade will be based on the number of points you obtain (and may also include extra credit points added to you total of points for research participation as described below or other surprise quizzes). The following table shows the points needed to obtain each grade level.

| Grade | Point Range | Percentage |
| --- | --- | --- |
| A | 306–340 | 90–100% |
| B | 272–305 | 80–89.9% |
| C | 238–271 | 70–79.9% |
| D | 204–237 | 60–69.9% |
| F | Below 204 | 59.9% and below |

If you would like to participate in experiments, you may earn bonus points that are added directly to the number of points you have earned from exams.

## Grade Dispute Procedures

After reviewing an exam and your grade with your TA, you may write a rebuttal on any item in which you believe your answer should be counted as correct. You must do this within **two** weeks of grades being posted. Your rebuttal must be typed. Please include your name, social security number, name and section of course, and the date, and indicate:

1. The item number and the form of the test you took;
2. The letter of the key answer;
3. The letter of your answer;
4. A paragraph **explaining** why you believe your answer should be counted as correct (caution: do not just complain, rather explain!).

Rebuttals that cite pages of the text or dates of the lectures prompting your answer will be given preference. Rebuttals are voluntary and compulsive students should avoid rebutting every question missed. If you recognize an answer as obviously wrong, do not write a rebuttal for it.

## Cheating

Instances of cheating will result in failure of the course and referral for disciplinary procedures, which may result in dismissal from the University.

## Participation in Experimental Studies

You may participate in psychological research for extra credit. In lectures and demonstrations I will try to teach you about the empirical procedures of psychology. However, by serving as a participant in psychological research you may gain insight into these procedures more fully than you could from class. The investigators have an obligation to help you learn from your participation by informing you about the procedures and the topic of the investigation as well as providing you with the opportunity to learn of the results of the study when it is completed. The studies that you may participate in will be conducted by faculty or advanced students; these people are serious about their attempts to advance our knowledge of human behavior. Your participation will therefore serve to augment your own knowledge about psychology as well as help the progress of the field of psychology. Each time you participate in a study, you will receive at least one point toward your final total of points. **You will not receive credit for more than five points worth of participation**, but you may participate in as many research opportunities as you like. The number of points you earn in any study depends upon the amount of time you devote to your participation (1 point is given for one hour of participation, but I will round .5 to 1 and 1.5 to 2 etc.). Opportunities for research participation are listed on the bulletin board in the basement of DeGarmo Hall.

Most of the experiments will not require any special background or skill on your part. You will only have to be there at the time you have signed up. **If you have to miss an appointment, make every attempt to get in touch with the experimenter beforehand.**

When your participation is over, the experimenter will give you a blue card. Fill it out completely with your name clearly printed. Give this card to your Graduate Assistant. Occasionally, experimenters have not been able to keep appointments and have not been able to notify their scheduled participants. If you go to an experiment and this happens, inform me as soon as possible. You will be given credit for having appeared.

Finally, a guardian must approve your participation in an experiment if you are under 18. This means that a legal guardian also has to sign the consent form that all of our research participants are required to sign. If you are under eighteen and want to participate in a particular study, go to the experimenter early, get a consent form, and send it home. Then, bring the signed form in with you at the time you are scheduled. **(See Handout 3.1.)**

You may find it useful to keep track of your grades by entering them in the spaces below:

| | | | |
|---|---|---|---|
| Quiz | _____ | Optional Final | _____ |
| Exam 1 | _____ | Total Points | _____ |
| Exam 2 | _____ | Research Pts. | _____ |
| Exam 3 | _____ | Extra Quiz Pts. | _____ |
| Exam 4 | _____ | Grand Total | _____ |
| Exam 5 | _____ | | |

See grading scale previously listed in this syllabus to determine point totals for various grades.

**Schedule**

| **Date** | | **Assigned Reading** |
|---|---|---|
| Week 1: | Mon, Aug 24 | Syllabus and Intro. |
| | Wed, Aug 26 | Chapter 1: Intro. to Psy. |
| | Fri, Aug 28 | Chapter 1: Continued |
| | | |
| Week 2: | Mon, Aug 31 | Chapter 2: Psych. Res. |
| | Wed, Sept 2 | Chapter 2: Psych. Res. |
| | **Fri, Sept 4** | **Quiz on Chap. 1 & 2** |
| | | Ethics in Research |
| | | |
| Week 3: | **Mon, Sept 7** | **Labor Day Holiday!** |
| | Wed, Sept 9 | Chapter 3: Bio. & Behav. |
| | Fri, Sept 11 | Chapter 3: Bio. (Con't) |
| | | |
| Week 4: | Mon, Sept 14 | Chapter 3: Bio. (Con't) |
| | Wed, Sept 16 | Chapter 4: Sensation |
| | Fri, Sept 18 | Chapter 4: Perception |
| | | |
| Week 5: | Mon, Sept 21 | Chapter 5: States of Con. |
| | Wed, Sept 23 | Chapter 5: (Con't) |
| | **Fri, Sept 25** | **EXAM 1: Chapters 3, 4, & 5** |
| | | |
| Week 6: | Mon, Sept 28 | Chapter 6: Learning: |
| | Wed, Sept 30 | Chapter 6: (Con't) |
| | Fri, Oct 2 | Chapter 6: (Con't) |
| | | |
| Week 7: | Mon, Oct 5 | Chapter 7: Memory |
| | Wed, Oct 7 | Chapter 7: Memory |
| | Fri, Oct 9 | Chapter 8: Cognition |
| | | |
| Week 8: | Mon, Oct 12 | Chapter 8: Language |
| | **Wed, Oct 14** | **EXAM 2: Chapters 6, 7, 8** |
| | **Fri, Oct 16** | **Fall Break Day!** |

## Schedule

| Date | | Assigned Reading |
|---|---|---|
| Week 9: | Mon, Oct 19 | Chapter 9: Intelligence |
| | Wed, Oct 21 | Chapter 9: Intelligence |
| | Fri, Oct 23 | Chapter 10: Motivation |
| Week 10: | Mon, Oct 26 | Chapter 10: Emotion |
| | Wed, Oct 28 | Chapter 11: Sexuality |
| | Fri, Oct 30 | Chapter 11: Gender |
| Week 11: | **Mon, Nov 2** | **EXAM 3: Chapters 9, 10, & 11** |
| | Wed, Nov 4 | Chapter 12: Development |
| | Fri, Nov 6 | Chapter 12: (Con't) |
| Week 12: | Mon, Nov 9 | Chapter 13: Adult Dev. |
| | Wed, Nov 11 | Chapter 14: Personality |
| | Fri, Nov 13 | Chapter 14: Personality |
| Week 13: | **Mon, Nov 16** | **Exam 4: Chapters 12, 13, & 14** |
| | Wed, Nov 18 | Chapter 15: Health Psych. |
| | Fri, Nov 20 | Chapter 15: (Con't) |
| Week 14: | Mon, Nov 23 | Chapter 16: Disorders |
| | Wed, Nov 25 | Chapter 16: (Con't) |
| | **Fri, Nov 27** | **Thanksgiving!** |
| Week 15: | Mon, Nov 30 | Chapter 17: Treatment |
| | Wed, Dec 2 | Chapter 17: Treatment |
| | Fri, Dec 4 | Chapter 18: Social Psych. |
| Week 16: | Mon, Dec 7 | Chapter 18: (Con't) |
| | Wed, Dec 9 | Chapter 18: (Con't) |
| | **Fri, Dec 11** | **EXAM 5: Chap. 15, 16, 17, & 18** |

**Tuesday Dec 15   OPTIONAL FINAL EXAM 7:50 A.M.**

Handout 3.1


---

**AUTHORIZATION TO POST GRADES**


Please sign the following so that your exam scores may be posted by Social Security number.

I, _____
                                                        Signature

(SS# _____), hereby authorize Dr. Patricia Jarvis and/or her Graduate Teaching Assistants to post any of my grades for examination results by Social Security Number for Psychology 111–Introductory Psychology during the present semester/Fall 1999. I am aware of my rights under the Family Educational Rights and Privacy Act of 1974 as amended, to prohibit the use of any personally identifiable information. However, I am granting authorization to post grades or results as a personal convenience and benefit.

---

# Chapter 4

# History of Psychology

> ## Putting Psychological Milestones Into an Historical Perspective

Students are often surprised to learn that psychology is considered a very young science. The following brief activity provides students with the chance to put some of the major milestones in psychology into perspective. The activity not only reinforces some of the important dates that students of psychology are expected to know, it also illustrates how the zeitgeist (spirit of the times) had an impact on the field of psychology. Students get a good grasp of how world events shaped events/research in psychology.

**DEMONSTRATION:** Students are provided with a timeline of major historical events on an overhead transparency. They are then given a list of milestones in psychology and asked to interweave these into the timeline.

**MATERIALS:**
- Two overhead transparencies (one prepared with historical dates outlined; the second with a list of important psychological milestones, see OHTs 4.1 and 4.2)
- One sheet of notebook paper per student

**TIME:** Approximately 15 minutes

**PROCEDURES:**

1. Before your lecture on the history of psychology, ask the students to take out a sheet of notebook paper.

2. Show the following timeline on an overhead transparency (**see OHT 4.1**). (Note: instructors may choose dates to coincide with the psychological milestones they would like to emphasize.)

a. 1776: The Declaration of Independence is signed.

b. 1861: Fort Sumpter is taken by the Confederacy, signaling the beginning of the Civil War.

c. 1919: The 19th Amendment to the Constitution is passed, giving women the right to vote.

d. 1939: Hitler invades Poland, signaling the beginning of WWII.

e. 1945: The Nuremberg Trials are held and Nazi war criminals are put on trial for crimes against humanity.

f. 1964: The U. S. Congress passes the Civil Rights Act protecting voting rights, opening access to all races, and providing all races equal opportunities in business and unions.

3. On a second transparency (**see OHT 4.2**), list the following in random order (without the dates).

a. Psychology is established as a science when Wilhelm Wundt founded the first psychological laboratory in Germany. **(1879)**

b. Kenneth Clark becomes the first African American to serve as the president of the American Psychological Association. **(1971)**

c. Margaret Washburn becomes the first woman to earn a Ph.D. in psychology. **(1908)**

d. Sigmund Freud publishes the **Interpretation of Dreams. (1900)**

e. Solomon Asch publishes his classic work on the nature of conformity. **(1951)**

4. Ask the students to interweave these events into the historical timeline.

5. Give the students the actual dates and let them check their accuracy. What tends to happen is that most students place the beginning of psychology at the beginning of the timeline. They find it difficult to believe that psychology as a science is just over a hundred years old. Similarly, most students find it hard to believe that Freud lived and wrote during the twentieth century. The brief history lesson also gives the instructor the chance to get across to students that events/research in psychology do not occur in an historical vacuum. The concerns and issues of the day shaped the milestones in our field and dictated the research that was of interest to psychologists. Instructors can add their own dates to this exercise. We like to ask students to describe what social events they associate with

each decade. If they had to guess, what research topics would have likely been of interest to psychologists during each particular decade (e.g., social psychological research on obedience, conformity, authoritarian personality, leadership following WWII, research on self-development and self-actualization during the 1950–60s; research exploring gender differences in the 1970s; etc.). Ask students what they think are hot topics for contemporary psychologists and psychologists of the future. Given what is going on societally, what would they think is important to research?

Historical Dates Outline

A.  1776:  The Declaration of Independence is signed.

B.  1861:  Fort Sumpter is taken by the Confederacy, signaling the beginning of the Civil War.

C.  1919:  The 19th Amendment to the Constitution is passed, giving women the right to vote.

D.  1939:  Hitler invades Poland, signaling the beginning of WWII.

E.  1945:  The Nuremberg Trials are held and Nazi war criminals are put on trial for crimes against humanity.

F.  1964:  The U.S. Congress passes the Civil Rights Act protecting voting rights, opening access to all races, and providing all races equal opportunities in business and unions.

# Important Psychological Milestones

A. Psychology is established as a science when Wilhelm Wundt founded the first psychological laboratory in Germany.

B. Kenneth Clark becomes the first African American to serve as the president of the American Psychological Association.

C. Margaret Washburn becomes the first woman to earn a Ph.D. in psychology.

D. Sigmund Freud publishes the *Interpretation of Dreams*.

E. Solomon Asch publishes his classic work on the nature of conformity.

| Introspection |
| :---: |

The following activity can be used to illustrate Wundt's technique of introspection. This brief activity helps students experience how Wundt measured consciousness. In addition, the activity can be used to discuss the shortcomings of introspection.

**DEMONSTRATION:** In pairs, students use the method of introspection to describe an object they have brought to class.

**MATERIALS:**
- Any object (e.g., pen or pencil, piece of fruit, newspaper, notebook)

**TIME:** Approximately 5 minutes

**PROCEDURES:**

1. Before introducing this exercise, familiarize students with the Structuralist approach to the study of psychology. In particular, explain that Wundt's primary goal was to understand the structure of our conscious mind. Then ask students how they would go about measuring a person's conscious experience of an object or event.

2. After discussing some of these approaches, describe Wundt's technique of introspection. Ask students to pick up some object that they have brought to class. Give some examples, like a pen, food, or newspaper.

3. Ask students to pair up with a person sitting next to them. Students take turns describing the objects by verbalizing the contents of their conscious minds. Make it clear that Wundt trained people to report on the experience of the object—sensations, feelings, and emotions, not on its name or function. Giving students an example is helpful.

4. Discuss the shortcomings of this method. Ask students if they had difficulty reporting only sensations, feelings, emotions, etc. How many of them thought about the function of the object? Other thoughts? Did Wundt unrealistically limit the content of the conscious mind? Does introspection reflect the way we experience objects and events? Do people experience objects and events as a series of sensations or as an integrated whole? Is there more to experience than conscious awareness?

# Pencil Envy: A Test of Freud's Theory

The following activity is based on research by Johnson (1966) and can be used to demonstrate unconscious motivation and Freud's concept of penis envy. Students find the activity humorous and it generates much discussion.

**DEMONSTRATION:** Students are loaned pencils to use on a quiz about their current knowledge of psychology. They are asked to return the pencils when they turn in their quiz answer sheets. The percentage of pencils returned by male versus female students are monitored. In most cases, a higher percentage of the male student will return their pencils.

**MATERIALS:**
- Pencils
- Short quiz with answer sheets

**TIME:** Approximately 15 minutes

**PROCEDURES:**

1. After presenting a brief introduction to the course, tell students that you will be giving them a short, non-graded quiz over the content area of psychology. The purpose of the quiz is for you to gauge their familiarity with the course material. At this time, pass out pencils to the class. It is helpful to have assistants help with this task.

2. When students have completed the quiz ask them to place their answer sheets in a pile at the front of the room and return their pencils to a box located next to the answer sheets.

3. Have two assistants unobtrusively monitor the percentage of males and females who return their pencils.

4. The results of the activity can be presented while introducing Freud in the History of Psychology lecture. When discussing Freud's ideas about the unconscious sexual drive—ask the students if they buy into Freud's ideas—did they have unconscious sexual desires for their opposite-sex parent? Do the males remember experiencing castration anxiety? Did the females experience penis envy? Many students will find Freud's ideas hard to believe.

5. Point out that Freud believed that our sexual drive was unconscious—so he wouldn't expect us to remember these feelings and desires. However, expressions of these urges should come out in hidden ways. For example, we may be attracted to objects that resemble sex organs (give some examples for both sexes). Then hold up a pencil—and say, for instance . . . report the results of the pencil activity—women are more likely to keep the pencil.

6. Tell the class that this may be the result of an unconscious desire to have a penis. This can lead to a discussion of alternative explanations (women are more dishonest, women have purses, etc.). Also, it is a good illustration of why Freud's theory is so difficult to test.

**Related Reading:**

Johnson, G. B. (1966). Penis envy or pencil needing? *Psychological Reports*, **19**, 758.

# Chapter 5

# Psychological Research

Scientific Method:
Why Psychologists Prefer the
Scientific Method as a Way of
Gathering Knowledge

Students learn about the scientific method in many of their courses. This activity can be useful as an introduction to psychology or it can be used when psychological research methodology is covered. We prefer to use it at the end of presenting information on the history of the discipline, but before we discuss methodology.

**DEMONSTRATION:** While many people accept controlled studies as a good way to obtain information, we are nevertheless sometimes susceptible to accepting untested propositions as truth. The following activity effectively demonstrates that psychologists (and other human beings) must be careful that the things they believe to be true are, in fact, accurate. Truth can be acquired in many ways, but the scientific method is perhaps the best way for psychologists to learn about behavior because it reduces the chances that this knowledge or truth will be based on inaccurate material.

**MATERIALS:**
- One sheet of notebook paper per student
- Overhead transparency 5.1

**TIME:** Approximately 20 minutes

**PROCEDURES:**

1. To demonstrate the tendency that we all have to accept information uncritically from others as truth, announce to the class that you will be giving them a brief lecture on the scientific method and that it will be followed by a short quiz. The quiz is included and can be put on a transparency. Base the lecture on the following information. The material in bold italics is **inaccurate** (but don't tell them that yet!).

**Lecture:**

A famous *German structuralist* philosopher by the name of *Edward Horton Sanders* wrote an essay entitled *"In Defense of Science"* over *two hundred years ago*, in which he argued that although humans have many different ways of gathering knowledge, the preferred way for approaching the truth is the scientific method.

How else can we gather knowledge about things? Sanders said that we learn much secondhand from authorities. For example, an expert authority tells you that something is true and, although he or she can be checked, you usually don't check for reasons of time and interest. When Susan takes her van to the mechanic and is told it needs new brakes, or when a dentist tells Stan he needs a cavity filled, these experts are usually believed without being checked. However, expert authorities such as these and others, like teachers, journalists, and physicians, can be wrong.

The scientific method, according to Sanders, by being public and self-corrective, provides a chance to detect errors and, through the requirement that any good piece of research much be replicated, also provides a chance to correct these errors. Suppose a researcher reports that depressed people blame themselves for bad outcomes even when they are not their fault. In order for this to be ultimately accepted by psychologists as being true, the researcher must report his or her procedures and findings in a public forum, such as a professional journal, where others can read and perhaps criticize them. If another independent researcher does the experiment over and finds essentially the same results, then people have more faith in it. If however, others fail to replicate the original work or do so in modified form, such as finding that the results are only true for females with depression, then the findings of the original study will likely be viewed skeptically by others.

The self-corrective nature of the scientific method is evident by the use of the technique itself, such as in controlled experiments, to try and test whether knowledge originally gained through the scientific method is accurate. Because this "correction factor" is not generally available for knowledge from authorities or common sense, these ways of acquiring knowledge are generally not endorsed by psychologists.

2. Administer the quiz on the next page (see **OHT 5.1**). You might xerox this quiz and then make an overhead transparency. It also can be given orally.

3. After students finish the quiz, tell them you will not grade it because although most of the lecture about the scientific method was accurate, the initial part (and the first three quiz questions) contained material that you just made up (expect a major class reaction at this point!). Go on to tell them that there was no German philosopher of the structuralist school named Edward Horton Sanders who lived about two hundred years ago and wrote an essay called "In Defense of Society."

Rather, confess that you made it up just to show how prone people are to accepting what others tell them as the truth. Psychologists need to be careful and depend on the scientific method as a preferred way to gather knowledge.

4. At this point, continue the discussion with a more detailed look at how the scientific method is used in psychology (observations, facts, hypotheses, theories, etc.). You might also want to point out that it was Charles Sanders Pierce, an American pragmatist philosopher, who wrote an essay entitled "The Fixation of Belief" about a hundred years ago in which he made these points. Don't be surprised if your students do not believe this or anything else that you say at this point!

Note: Author unknown.

**Scientific Method Quiz**

1. Who wrote "In Defense of Science"? _____

2. When was this influential essay written? _____

3. What school of philosophy did the author of the essay subscribe to?
   _____

4. When we learn things from others, what is this way of gathering knowledge called?
   _____

5. What two features of the scientific method make it preferable as a way of gathering knowledge for psychologists?

   A. _____
   B. _____

6. If an experiment is successfully repeated by another researcher, we say that it has been _____.

# Correlation Versus Research

This activity is an old standby that has been described in various forms in numerous teaching manuals. It can be adapted to large class sizes and works quite well to illustrate the difference between correlation and causation. In addition, the activity can be used to introduce the need for experimental research in psychology. Alternative explanations for data and confounds of studies can be considered, as well. Finally, information on hypothesis testing and independent and dependent variables can be presented.

**DEMONSTRATION:** In small groups (2–3 students per group) students determine the legitimacy of conclusions drawn from observations. Their opinions are then discussed in the larger lecture setting.

**MATERIALS:**
- Handout 5.1 describing an observation and subsequent conclusion

**TIME:**
Approximately 10–15 minutes for small group discussion followed by a 15–minute class discussion.

**PROCEDURES:**

1. Prepare a handout containing 5–6 observations and subsequent conclusions (**see example Handout 5.1** for ideas). Try to choose observations that reflect different content areas of psychology (e.g., developmental, social, physiological).

2. Begin the class period by passing out the handout. Tell students that you would like them to discuss the observations and conclusions given on the handout with a student or two sitting next to them. Ask the groups to decide if the conclusion is sound based on the information given in the observation. If the conclusion is not sound, the students should provide reasons why the statement is not warranted. Give the class 10–15 minutes to discuss the handout in their small groups.

3. Stop the groups after 10–15 minutes so that the class can discuss the observations and conclusions as a whole. Start with the first observation and, by a show of hands, ask how many of the groups agreed with the conclusion. Then ask those students who do not think the conclusion was warranted to explain their rationale. Do this for all the observations and conclusions. Use these responses to illustrate that these observations imply only correlation, not causation. Discuss the alternative explanations the class gave for each of the observations. Discuss what is necessary to make causal conclusions leading the class to information on the experimental method.

4. Have the students return to each of the examples and generate an experimental hypothesis to test the conclusion. Identify independent and dependent variables for each hypothesis.

**Handout 5.1**

---

## Observations And Conclusions

Read each of the following observations. Assume that the observations were accurately observed. Next read the conclusion made based on the observation. Is this conclusion warranted? If not, why not?

1. **OBSERVATION:** A physiological psychologist observes that people with higher levels of the neurotransmitter, dopamine, exhibit more behaviors associated with schizophrenia than those with lower levels of dopamine.

   **CONCLUSION:** High dopamine levels cause schizophrenia.

2. **OBSERVATION:** A psychologist studying sensation and perception observes that blue eyed subjects make more mistakes when interpreting visual stimuli than do subjects with brown eyes.

   **CONCLUSION:** The color of the iris determines how well we perceive visual stimuli.

3. **OBSERVATION:** A developmental psychologist notices that male and female children prefer different toys during their preschool years. In particular, girls enjoy playing with dolls and stuffed animals while boys like action figures and guns.

   **CONCLUSION:** Males and females have innate biological differences. Females are more nurturing and males are more aggressive.

4. **OBSERVATION:** A social psychologist observes that older people with pets live longer than older people without pets.

   **CONCLUSION:** If people want to live longer, they should have a pet.

5. **OBSERVATION:** An industrial/organizational psychologist observes that people who are most satisfied with their jobs perform at higher levels than people who are dissatisfied.

   **CONCLUSION:** Job satisfaction causes performance.

---

The following activity is based on an exercise developed by David Watson to illustrate random assignment to groups. Typically students have a difficult time understanding this concept without a concrete example. The activity also can be expanded to incorporate the concept of meta-analytic techniques. Students typically find the material on experimental methods a little dry. This activity is a good way of breaking up the material while at the same time illustrating some important experimental design principles.

**DEMONSTRATION:** A volunteer from the class assigns class members to groups using random assignment.

**MATERIALS:**
- 24 volunteers
- 24 poker chips or colored pieces of paper (12 each in two different colors)

**TIME:** Approximately 20 minutes

**PROCEDURES:**

1. Before beginning this activity, discuss random assignment with the class. Explain that random assignment involves assigning participants to conditions in such a way that every participants has the same chance of being place in any of the experimental conditions. Describe how random assignment can be implemented (e.g., random number table, flipping a coin, drawing slips of paper from a hat, etc.). Lead the class in a discussion of how random assignment is an important means of controlling for the effects of any pre-existing differences among participants (e.g., gender, height, weight, intelligence levels, etc.) that may impact the relationship between the independent and dependent variables. Remind the class that through random assignment the experimental conditions are roughly equivalent except for the independent variable.

2. Tell the class that you have developed a superior coaching technique in basketball and would like to test the effectiveness of your method via an experiment. One team (the control group) will be coached using traditional methods; the other team (the experimental group) will be trained using your new technique. If your coaching technique is, in fact, superior, the experimental group should perform better than the control group in a basketball game.

3.  Explain to the class that you are concerned about controlling for height—a key variable in basketball. If all the tall players wind up on the control team, the experimental team might lose the game and the loss might be chalked up to the ineffectiveness of your coaching technique rather than the real culprit—the superior height of the control team.

4.  Tell the class that you will randomly assign players to the two teams through random assignment. Watson recommends using only one gender in this activity since there is so much variation in height.

5.  Randomly approach members of the class and have them pick out a poker chip or slip of paper from a hat. All blue chips/slips go to Team A and all red chips/slips are assigned to Team B. Have students stand on different sides of the room once they have been assigned.

6.  Assign 3 members to each team. Ask each team member their height. Convert heights to inches. Have the rest of the class figure out the number of inches associated with each team. With only three members, what typically happens is that there is still a lot a variability between groups due to the small sample size and the influence of outliers. Assign three more members to each group. Have the class re-compute the number of inches. What you will tend to see is the discrepancy between groups dwindling. Assign six more members to each team (12 per each team now). Have the class re-compute the number of inches associated with each team. Once again, you will typically see a reduction in the height discrepancy between teams. For visual confirmation, Watson recommends having each team line up from shortest to tallest to illustrate how height has been successfully randomized out across experimental conditions.

7.  Ask class members why random assignment was not successful when it was used with only three members per team. The class will bring up the role of outliers, etc. Remind the class that even though random assignment is a powerful experimental tool to control for experimental confounds, it is not a panacea. An experimenter needs the advantage of the "law of large numbers" in order for random assignment to be truly effective. Lead the class in a discussion of how experiments with a small sample size (even those that utilized random assignment) may lead to erroneous conclusions. Describe how researchers try to counteract this small sample size problem by statistically combining the samples of numerous experiments that have investigated the same phenomenon (i.e., a meta-analysis). Using meta-analytic procedures, researchers may end up with sample sizes in the thousands and the problems associated with any one study (coding errors, data entry errors, unreliable measures, etc.) are minimized. The researcher can determine an "average effect" for the phenomenon.

**Related Reading:**

Watson, D. (1990). A neat little demonstration of the benefits of random assignment of subjects in an experiment. In V. P. Makosky, C. C. Sileo, L. G. Whittemore, C. P. Landry, & M. L. Skutley (Eds.) **Activities handbook for the teaching of psychology**: Vol. **3** (p. 4). Washington, DC: American Psychological Association.

# Chapter 6

# Biology and Behavior

Reaction-Time Measure of
Neural Transmission
and Mental Processes

(Adapted from Rozin & Jonides, 1977)

The following activity illustrates an important principle of neural transmission and is best conducted after the basic principles of neuronal transmission are covered in lecture. In addition, it is fun and loosens up the class in the stiff early days of the term.

**DEMONSTRATION:** Students form a neural chain and transmit a nerve impulse under timed conditions.

**MATERIALS:**
- Two stop watches or wristwatches with second hands or digital watches that show seconds

**TIME:** Approximately 10–15 minutes

**PROCEDURES:**

1. Begin by having students in the front two rows and the back two rows of the lecture hall form two chains by putting their right hand on the shoulder of the person in front of them. Students will need to turn to their right to have the chains snake from one row to the other. Stand behind the first person in the chain in the front of the class with a stopwatch or a watch with a second hand or a digital watch that shows seconds. Have a graduate assistant or a volunteer student stand behind the first person of the row in the back of the lecture hall.

2. Instruct students in the chains that you and your "assistant" will be squeezing the shoulder of the first student in the chain after which that student must squeeze the same shoulder of the next student in the chain and so forth throughout the chains.

3. Start your watches timing as you squeeze the shoulder of the first student. After sending your "message" move to the end of the chain and stop the timers when your own shoulders are squeezed.

4. When conducted in a large lecture hall with two chains of students consisting of about 30 students each, the chain in the front of the class takes about 8 seconds on the first try. The chain in the back of the lecture hall takes about 10 seconds (ask the class why). With a second try, each chain can shave a few seconds off of their time, but there usually is still a discrepancy between the time for the two chains. Discuss the process of neural transmission, including reaction time differences for those sitting closer to the message source (the Professor) versus those sitting in the back of the lecture hall. (Note: This is a good opportunity to encourage students to sit closer to the front of the room if they are having difficulty getting all the lecture notes and keeping up with the pace of the lectures.)

5. Next, have students take their seats and consider whether they would expect a faster, slower, or similar time if instead they squeezed the ankle of the person to their right. From lecture and text material, most should be able to reason that it should take longer to feel the squeeze, because the sensory input has further to travel (from the ankle versus the shoulder). Try it and indeed it will take a bit longer. This provides an example of the speed of neural transmission.

6. Next, have students stand again and this time grab both shoulders of the person in front. Tell them to squeeze whichever shoulder is squeezed (timers may randomly select which shoulder to squeeze at the beginning of the chains). This takes about 10 seconds. This illustrates how a simple reaction-time measure can assess the speed of cognitive processing (compare to how long it takes people to react to stoplights changing from red to green and get their car going).

7. Finally, ask for a more demanding task. Have students squeeze the shoulder opposite the one squeezed on them of the next person in the chain—such that if your right shoulder was squeezed, squeeze the left shoulder of the next person (neuron). Times will reveal that reaction time is a function of complexity of the message to be processed (have the class imagine how much longer it would take drivers if they had to do the opposite of what the traffic light indicated and go on red or stop on green).

**Related Reading:**

Rozin, P., and Jonides, J. (1977). Mass reaction time measurement of the speed of the nerve impulse and the duration of mental processes in class. *Teaching of Psychology*, **4** (2), 91–94.

# Hemispheric Specialization

Several demonstrations have been developed to illustrate hemispheric specialization (for other examples, see Kemble, Filipi, & Gravlin, 1985). This particular activity is based on the Stroop Test (1935) and works well in a large classroom setting. Students will find that processing written information (primarily a left brain task) takes less time than naming colors (primary a right brain task). In addition, a task that requires the students to name the color of ink (e.g., blue) used to write the name of a different color (e.g., green) is quite difficult.

**DEMONSTRATION:** Two or three volunteer students are asked to: 1) read a list of color names printed in black ink; 2) name a series of color splotches; and 3) name the color of ink used to write a color name. Another student will be asked to record the time spent on each of the three tasks.

**MATERIALS:**
- Two or three volunteers
- Transparencies depicting examples from the Stroop Test

**TIME:** Approximately 10–15 minutes

**PROCEDURES:**

1. Before lecturing on hemispheric specialization, present this activity to students. They find it involving and fun.

2. Ask for two or three volunteers to come up in front of the class and read what is presented on the overhead projector. Also ask another student to serve as the official timer. Explain the exercise to the students in steps. First, present a list of color names presented in black ink (see **OHT 6.1**). Ask each volunteer student to read through the list, while the timer records the time taken to complete the task. Second, present the overhead containing color swatches (to make this transparency, photocopy **OHT 6.2** and fill each box with a different color, using markers). Ask each student to name each of the colors. Again, have the timer record the length of time needed to complete the task. Students will take longer to complete the second task. Ask the class why the second task is more difficult.

3. Third, present the final overhead. This overhead should be based upon **OHT 6.3**, however, each word should be presented in different colored ink, not black ink. Also, each word should be printed with a color other than the color that each word represents. For example, the word "blue" should be printed with green ink and the word "yellow" should be printed with red ink. Present this overhead to the students and ask each student to go through the list of color words and name the color of ink used to print the word. Again record the time. Students will have a difficult time and this task will take considerably longer than the first two. Identify the kinds of errors the students make. When they read the word rather than

name the color of the ink. Ask students why this task is difficult. This leads to a discussion of hemispheric specialization.

**Related Reading:**

Kemble, E.D., Filipi, T., & Gravlin, L. (1985). Some simple classroom experiments on cerebral lateralization. *Teaching of Psychology*, **12**, 81–83.

MacLeod, C. M. (1991). Half a century of research on the Stroop effect: An integrative review. *Psychological Bulletin*, **109**, 163–203.

Stoop, J. R. (1935). Studies of interference in serial verbal reactions. *Journal of Experimental Psychology*, **18**, 643–662.

# Read the List of Words

| | |
|---|---|
| Blue | Orange |
| Green | Blue |
| Red | Green |
| Yellow | Purple |
| Red | Brown |
| Orange | Green |
| Green | Yellow |
| Brown | Red |
| Yellow | Green |
| Purple | Brown |
| Red | Orange |

# Name the Color of the Ink

# Name the Color of the Ink

| Blue | Orange | Purple | Green |
|------|--------|--------|-------|
| Green | Green | Brown | Brown |
| Red | Brown | Green | Orange |
| Yellow | Yellow | Yellow | |
| | Purple | | |
| | Red | | |
| | Orange | | |
| | blue | | |
| | Blue | | |

# Chapter 7

# Sensation and Perception

## Demonstrating Binocular Vision

### (Adapted from Fisher, 1979)

The following brief activity illustrates the phenomenon of binocular vision. Binocular vision allows us to see three-dimensional images due to the combined effort of both of our eyes. In the following illusion, students focus on two images and with appropriate movement the two images fuse together due to the concerted effort of both eyes. Students enjoy this activity and it involves the entire class.

**DEMONSTRATION:** Students project different images on the retinas of both eyes. Due to binocular vision, the two images blend yielding a rather neat illusion.

**MATERIALS:**
- One page of notebook paper per student

**TIME**: Approximately 2 minutes

**PROCEDURES:**

1. This activity works well when discussing the binocular and monocular cues we use as a means of making judgments about depth.

2. Ask students to take out a sheet of notebook paper and roll it into a tube.

3. Students should hold the tube in their right hand and look through it with their right eye as if looking through a telescope. Ask students to focus on the wall in front of them as they look through the tube of paper.

4. Then ask students to hold up their left hand with the palm facing them. The edge of their left hand should be resting against the edge of the tube.

5. While still looking at the wall through the tube, students should move their left hand toward their face.

6. Both images will begin to fuse and students will see one image—that of a hole seemingly appearing in the middle of their hand!

## Related Reading:

Fisher, J. (1979). **Body Magic.** New York: Stein & Day Publishers.

---

# Sound Location

**(Adapted from Fisher, 1979)**

---

Just as binocular cues help one perceive depth in a three-dimensional world, binaural cues (i.e., information that reaches both ears) helps one locate sounds in the environment.

**DEMONSTRATION:** This is an amusing demonstration to illustrate the principle of binaural hearing.

**MATERIALS:**
- A volunteer with self-reported "good" hearing, a blindfold, and two coins or a noise-making clicker from a board game (ask students ahead of time if they have one of these you may borrow for a demonstration).

**TIME:** Approximately 10 minutes

**PROCEDURES:**

1. Ask the volunteer to sit blindfolded in a seat in the center of the front of the lecture hall.

2. Ask the volunteer to keep his or her head perfectly still and tell the student you will be asking him or her to judge the location of sounds you will make by pointing in the direction of the correct location of the sound.

3. Using a pair of coins rubbed together or the noise-making clicker from a board game, create sounds from a variety of randomly placed positions around the volunteer.

4. Although the volunteer should have no trouble locating noises made off to their right or left, they will invariably be way off the mark when the sound comes from the center (e.g., from between their knees, under their chin, or between their eyes).

5. Excuse the volunteer and thank him or her for helping with this activity.

6. Explain to the class that binaural cues are those that reach both ears. Tell them that when sounds come from anywhere other than straight ahead or straight behind us, the ear nearer to the sound source will perceive the noise slightly sooner and as slightly louder than will the opposite ear. Although the discrepancy in time and relative loudness is extremely small, the brain is able to use this information to accurately locate the sound.

**Related Reading:**

Fisher, J. (1979). **Body Magic**. Briarcliff Manor, NY: Stein & Day.

## Count the F's

This exercise serves as a good lecture launcher and gets students involved in the material studied in the sensation and perception chapters. In addition, it can be used to illustrate: how sensation differs from perception; that perception is a subjective process; and that perception is influenced by the context, as well as our experiences, motivations, and expectations.

**DEMONSTRATION:** Students read a brief passage on an overhead transparency or power point slide and then count the number of F's in the passage.

**MATERIALS:**

- Transparency (see OHT 7.1)
- One volunteer

**TIME:** Approximately 10 minutes

**PROCEDURES:**

1. At the onset of the sensation and perception lecture, ask students to read (to themselves) the following passage displayed on an overhead projector (**see OHT 7.1**).

> Finished files are the
> results of years of
> scientific study
> combined with the
> experiences of years.

2. Once they have had an opportunity to read the passage, ask them to go back and count the number of F's in the sentence. Then ask how many students counted three F's (several will raise their hands), then four F's, and so on. You will find that the majority of students do not count all six F's contained in the passage.

3. At this point, several students will still be trying to find all six F's. From this group ask for a volunteer to come up in front of the class and point to each of the F's on the overhead. In almost all cases, the student will pass over one or more of the F's and the class will laugh. The student then sees the F's that he/she had missed. These F's are usually part of the word "of."

4. The class then is asked to brainstorm reasons why the student (or they, themselves) may have passed over these F's. They typically generate the following reasons: the F's are in words with only two letters, the F's are part of words that are not related to the content of the message, the F's are pronounced with the "V" sound, etc.

5. At this point, explain how sensation is the process of taking in the information from the environment. Sensation is a rather objective process, so they probably sensed all six F's. Perception, on the other hand, is relatively subjective. This means that they perceived the F's based on the overall context and on their own motivations, expectations, etc. For example, based on past experience and expectation, they probably expect an F to sound like an F rather than a "V". So when they heard the "V" sound, they expected to see a V and therefore did not count that particular F.

Note: Author unknown.

**Related Reading:**

Diekhoff, G. M. (1987). The role of expectancies in the perception of language. In **Activities handbook for the teaching of psychology** (Vol. **2**). Washington, DC: American Psychological Association .

**FINISHED FILES ARE THE**

**RESULTS OF YEARS OF**

**SCIENTIFIC STUDY**

**COMBINED WITH THE**

**EXPERIENCES OF YEARS.**

## Understanding Weber's Law

**(Adapted from Coren, Ward, & Ennis, 1999)**

This activity is a simple demonstration of Ernst Weber's Law for perception of heaviness.

**DEMONSTRATION:** This activity demonstrates Weber's principle that difference thresholds grow with the magnitude of the stimulus. It is most useful to present this activity after explaining difference thresholds and Weber's Law. It is a good example of Weber's Law.

**MATERIALS:**
- Three volunteers
- Three quarters
- Two identical envelopes
- The largest pair of shoes available in class
- (Students can provide these materials on the spot.)

**TIME:** Approximately 10 minutes

**PROCEDURES:**

1. Ask for three volunteers (A, B, & C). Have one of them (A) place one quarter in one envelope and the remaining two quarters in the other envelope.

2. Have each of the other two volunteers (B & C) hold each of the two envelopes (one in each hand), respectively, and report to the class which one is heavier.

3. Ask volunteers B & C to turn their backs to volunteer A. Have volunteer A put each envelope in each shoe so that the other volunteers will not know which is which.

4. Ask volunteers B and C to turn around and lift the shoes one at a time and indicate if there is any weight difference between the two (they should not be able to perceive a difference).

5. Thank the volunteers and have them return to their seats.

6. Explain to the class that according to Weber, a change in a stimulus can only be judged after considering what the original level or value of the stimulus was or, in other words, differences grow as the magnitude of a stimulus grows.

**Related Reading:**

Coren, S., Ward, L. M., and Ennis, J. T. (1999). **Sensation and perception** (5th Edition). Fort Worth: Harcourt Brace.

# Chapter 8

# States of Consciousness

## Dream Interpretations

**(Adapted from Singer & Switzer, 1980)**

Many students are interested in understanding more about their states of consciousness. Specifically, students often wonder what their dreams mean in psychological terms. Our students have reported this activity on dream interpretation to be very interesting to them personally and it helps them master the course material on dream interpretation better.

**DEMONSTRATION:** This activity, adapted from Singer and Switzer, offers students an opportunity to keep track of their daydreams (which are more controllable and conscious than nighttime dreams) and interpret them. While this activity does not take place in class (unlike the other activities in this manual), it is worth taking a few minutes of class time to offer it to students as an explanation of how to interpret their dreams, as it is an application of the course material on latent and manifest content of dreams.

**MATERIALS:**
- Students will need to keep a "diary" of their dreams on a pad of paper or 3 x 5 cards they provide

**TIME:** Approximately 10 minutes of class time are needed to present this activity and describe how to interpret the "data" students can collect on themselves

**PROCEDURES:**

1. Present material on dreams as part of consciousness (including discussion of the Freudian concepts of latent and manifest content of dreams).

2. Next, tell students to keep track of their daydreams (pointing out that daydreams are more controllable and conscious than dreams occurring while one is asleep) over the next few days and you will explain how they might interpret the meaning of such dreams after that time.

3. Tell students to record their daytime fantasies over the next two or three days by carrying a pad of paper or 3 × 5 cards and during idle moments of the day—before class, waiting for the bus, during a coffee break etc.—and recalling and briefly recording fantasies or what they have just been thinking about.

4. Wait a few days (or lectures) before offering the following information on interpretation of dreams for this activity. We usually offer this activity to our students at the end of a class and then present the information on interpretation of dreams at the beginning of our next lecture (which is either two or three days later as we either teach our classes on Mondays, Wednesdays, and Fridays, or on Tuesdays and Thursdays).

5. To understand the meaning of their dreams, tell students to first look for certain specific attributes. For example do certain scenes and themes recur? These recurring themes would have greater meaning than isolated fantasies that only occur once or twice.

6. Next, tell students that Jerome Singer, the original author of this activity, suggests scoring daydreams from 1 to 5 on the following characteristics:

   a. Is the fantasy purely visual or do other senses come into play? For example, in fantasizing about a banquet do you hear the speaker, smell the food, taste the chicken? Some daydreams consist entirely of conversations with another person. Do you see the person and listen to his or her comments or do you simply do all the talking? Score a 1 if only one sense is involved but up to 5 if more senses come into play.

   b. Are your dreams personal or impersonal? In dreaming about a bank robbery, are you a spectator or are you actively involved as a perpetrator or victim? Score a 1 if you are merely a bystander and up to 5 if you are actively involved.

   c. Was the dream relevant to your real life? If you dream about visiting the harem of an Arabian sheik, you may be seeking escape from your daily problems. However, if you are rehearsing a conversation you will have with your professor tomorrow, you are dealing with an immediately relevant aspect of your life. Again score a 1 to 5 with 5 representing extreme, obvious relevance to your current life situation.

   d. How vivid was your dream? Did you see it through a thick fog or was it clear and sharp? Were events in color or black and white? Could you clearly hear what was being said? Score from 1 to 5, with higher scores representing more vivid experiences.

   Tell students to average their ratings for a whole series of dreams to obtain a sense of their underlying motives. For example, they may determine the extent to which their fantasies reflect their need to achieve. If they have not been doing well in school and telling themselves that it does not matter, while their daydreams show them overcoming incredible obstacles, they may have misjudged their deepest wishes. Similarly, if their daydreams consist of passionate love affairs, while in everyday life they have focused on success in school or career, they may be suppressing a deep need for affection. Students may want to assess the roles of power, dependency, escape from danger, etc. in their dreams. In each case, students should consider whether their dreams coincide with real-life efforts and goals or are very different from their real life affairs. If their dreams differ from their real life a great deal, students may be hiding certain motives from themselves and need to reevaluate their life efforts, according to Singer.

## Related Reading:

Singer, J., and Switzer, E. (1980). **Mind-Play.** Englewood Cliffs, NJ: Prentice-Hall.

---

# Where Did I Hear That Before?
# Creating a Déjà Vu Experience

**(Adapted from Appleby, 1987)**

---

The following activity, based on one written by Appleby (1987), is a fun demonstration of the frequently reported déjà vu experience. When the lecture turns to a discussion of dreams, many students report that they believe that they have has dreams of places and events and then subsequently actually found themselves in that exact place or situation. Such reports tie in well with déjà vu experiences (the illusion that one has previously had an experience). This free recall activity generates a déjà vu experience in a majority of students and helps them see that such experiences can be easily explained through empiricism rather than resorting to supernatural explanations.

**DEMONSTRATION:** Students are exposed to a variety of words in a free recall task, many of which have to do with sleeping. Later, when asked to recall the words, when students are asked whether they recalled hearing the word "sleep," many will think they have since many of the words were related to sleep. In actuality, however, "sleep" is not one of the words on the list.

**MATERIALS:**
- Word List (on a prepared overhead, **see OHT 8.1**)
- One page of notebook paper per student

**TIME:** Approximately 10 minutes

## PROCEDURES:

1. Announce to students that they are going to participate in a free recall demonstration. DO NOT MENTION THAT THE MEMORY TEST HAS TO DO WITH DÉJÀ VU.

2. **Using OHT 8.1**, show students each of the following 12 words on an overhead (one at a time). As you reveal each word, say it out loud as well. (REST, TIRED, AWAKE, DREAM, SNORE, BED, EAT, SLUMBER, SOUND, COMFORT, WAKE, NIGHT)

3. When the last word has been presented, ask the class to write down as many of the words as they can remember.

4. Give students approximately two minutes to write down what they can remember.

5. After they are finished, ask for a show of hands how many recalled the word? "AARDVARK" and then a separate show of hands for those that remembered the word "SLEEP."

6. When you ask about "AARDVARK" students will look at you as if you are deranged since they know that word was not on the list. However, the majority of the class (approximately 80%) of the class will raise their hands when you ask them if they recalled the word, "SLEEP." Those who did not have it on their list will look sheepish for not remembering such an such an easy word from the list.

7. Go through the list of actual words with the class. The class will be amazed to see that neither AARDVARK nor SLEEP appears on the list. Ask them why so many students thought **sleep** was on the list. They will respond with the explanation that many of the other words were related to it in some way.

8. Discuss with students how this experience can help explain how associations can lead a person to feel that an event has happened when in actuality it has not. Relate this experience to students' dreams. Many students believe that their dreams have predicted an event before it has actually occurred. Try to impress upon students that it makes more sense to look for the simple explanation based on naturally-occurring phenomena rather than complicated, supernatural or occult reasons for human behavior. The instructor also might bring up the X-Files TV show in which the Scully character is always trying to get the Mulder character to look for the simple, scientific explanation first.

**Related Readings:**

Appleby, D. (1987). Producing a déjà vu experience. In **Activities Handbook for the teaching of psychology** (Vol. **2**). Washington, DC: American Psychological Association.

Deese, J. (1959). On the occurrence of particular verbal intrusions in immediate recall. *Journal of Experimental Psychology*, **58**, 17–22.

# WORD LIST

REST

TIRED

AWAKE

DREAM

SNORE

BED

EAT

SLUMBER

SOUND

COMFORT

WAKE

NIGHT

# Demonstrating Suggestibility

This activity illustrates the concept of hypnotic suggestibility. Some students believe that hypnosis is a sham and that only the weak-minded can become vulnerable to the suggestions of others. We like using this brief activity as a way of reminding students of their own suggestibility.

**DEMONSTRATION:** Students listen to a vivid description of a scenario that generates physiological reactions.

**MATERIALS:** None

**TIME:** Approximately 10 minutes

**PROCEDURES:**

1. Have students close their eyes and visualize as you describe the following scenario.

2. Read the following description to students:

   Imagine that it is a hot sultry day in August. You have just come in from outside. You are hot and your throat is parched. You reach into the refrigerator and pull out a lemon. The lemon is bright yellow, plump and almost bursting with juice. You cut a wedge off of the lemon and bite into it. The acidic juices of the lemon flood your mouth. Some of the juices escape, trickling down your chin. The sourness of the lemon almost takes your breath away. Your cheeks pucker and your eyes begin to water due to the tartness. The juices of the lemon mingle with your saliva coating your mouth. You swallow convulsively trying to rid your mouth of the sour taste.

3. Pause and then ask students to open their eyes. Ask them to describe what they experienced as they visualized your description of the lemon. Did their mouths begin to pucker? Did they begin to salivate? Swallow convulsively?

4. Tie this into a discussion of hypnotic suggestibility. Remind students that whatever physiological reactions they experienced came about through mere words. Explain to students how some people are more easily hypnotized than others. Describe how about 10-20% of the population seem very susceptible to hypnotic suggestion while about 10% of the population cannot be hypnotized at all (Hilgard, 1965). Explain how those who may be more prone to hypnotic suggestions are those who show the capacity to immerse themselves in activities that require imagination (e.g., reading a

book, listening to music, etc.). Get the class further involved by asking if anyone has been hypnotized. Have the class member describe his/her experience.

5. Instructors also might tie this activity into a discussion of television commercials. Point out to the class that many commercials (e.g., fast food commercials, soft drink commercials) use imagery and vivid descriptions to generate physiological reactions (i.e., hunger, thirst, etc.) in the viewing public.

**Related Readings:**

Hilgard, E. R. (1965). **Hypnotic suggestibility.** New York: Harcourt Brace.

Fisher, J. (1979). **Body Magic.** Briarcliff Manor, NY: Stein & Day.

# Chapter 9

# Learning

Classically Conditioning
An Eyeblink Response

The following activity illustrates the learning principles associated with classical conditioning. One student will classically condition an eyeblink response in another student. This activity is a useful way of reinforcing the material on classical conditioning. Students really enjoy this activity. An additional benefit of this activity is that it helps students get a handle on some of the fairly difficult terminology involved in the classical conditioning paradigm.

**DEMONSTRATION:** One student will serve as a volunteer and classically condition an eyeblink response in another student.

**MATERIALS:**
- Three extroverted students to serve as volunteers
- A drinking straw
- A whistle (buzzer or something to make a loud noise)
- An overhead on which the linkages in the classical conditioning trial are given

**TIME:** Approximately 30 minutes

**PROCEDURES:**

1. This activity works best after lecturing on Pavlov's classical conditioning paradigm. After reviewing the linkages in Pavlov's research, tell the class that they are going to try to classically condition an eyeblink response. The basic paradigm you will be following is below and on the next page (to use to make an overhead transparency). We typically ask the class a series of questions as the activity unfolds so that the class fills in the linkages in a classical conditioning trial.

65

| A. Puff of Air (UCS) | ---------> | Eyeblink (UCR) |
| B. Loud Noise (Neutral Stimulus) | ---------> | Orienting Response |
| C. Puff of Air (UCS) + Loud Noise | ---------> | Eyeblink (UCR) |
| D. Loud Noise (CS) | ---------> | Eyeblink (CR) |

2. Solicit three volunteers from class. Ask the class what happens when someone blows a puff of air into one's eyes. Have the students demonstrate; ask to one student to blow a puff of air into the other students' eye using the straw. Ask the class whether this relationship constitutes an unconditioned relationship (naturally occurring, unlearned) or a conditioned (learned) relationship. Remind students that this is a reliable, naturally occurring phenomenon that does not need to be learned. (Ask the class to provide the first linkage before revealing it on the overhead transparency.)

3. Now ask students what happens when they hear a loud noise? Students probably will respond by saying that you pay attention or orient toward the sound. Ask the third volunteer to make the loud noise. Remind them that our typical response to a loud noise is not an eyeblink—thus using Pavlovian terminology, a loud noise would be a neutral stimulus. (Ask for the second linkage on the overhead transparency.)

4. Now ask the class how we can engender an eyeblink response to a loud noise in a person. Students should respond that, as with Pavlov, you could pair a loud noise with a puff of air over repeated trials. After multiple trials, the person should blink his/her eye upon just hearing the noise. (Ask for the third linkage on the overhead transparency.)

5. Tell the class that by using multiple trials, the class is going to try to get the volunteer to learn the association. One student should make the noise followed immediately by the second volunteer blowing a puff of air into your third volunteer's eye. At this point, we usually talk about the appropriate time lag between the noise and the puff of air in order for efficient conditioning to occur. Remind the class that the response (eyeblink) is still an unconditioned response as the unconditioned stimulus is present. Tell the volunteer making the noise that after ten trials, they should make the noise while tapping the "straw" volunteer on the shoulder. The shoulder tap will signal to the "straw" volunteer that this is the experimental trial and he/she should not blow a puff of air through the straw.

6. Lead the class in a series of trials (approximately 10) with the loud noise paired with the puff of air. A warning here . . . your volunteers tend to get a tad giggly at this point. We play along by reminding them in a stern voice that they must be objective scientists . . . dispassionate . . . dedicated to their research. The class loves this!

7. After the tenth trial, the person making the loud noise should tap the "straw volunteer" on the shoulder as he/she makes the noise. The "straw" volunteer should refrain from blowing through the straw. If conditioning has been successful, your first volunteer should blink in response to the noise. Ask the class if the eyeblink in response to the loud noise is a learned

or unlearned relationship. After they have responded, put up/fill in the last linkage in the paradigm. Remind students that the previously neutral stimulus is now a learned stimulus and the response it generates also is a learned response. If conditioning is not successful, ask the students why it wasn't (too long a time lapse between neutral stimulus and unconditioned stimulus, not enough trials, recalcitrant volunteers, etc.). (Ask for the fourth linkage on the overhead transparency.)

8. Lead the class in a round of applause for your volunteers.

9. Discuss with the class other principles of classical conditioning. Ask them for an example of how stimulus generalization might occur (if your volunteer is blinking to any loud noise . . . siren, telephone, etc.). Ask the class how you can get the volunteer to only blink in response to a certain noise (i.e., stimulus discrimination). Finish by asking for their help in getting extinction to occur (so that your volunteer does not go through life blinking like a mad person in response to loud noises).

# Classical Conditioning Paradigm

A. Puff of Air (UCS)    ---------> Eyeblink (UCR)

B. Loud Noise           ---------> Orienting Response
   (Neutral Stimulus)

C. Puff of Air (UCS) (CS)              ---------> Eyeblink (CR)
   + Loud Noise

D. Loud Noise (CS)    ---------> Eyeblink (CR)

# Learning Through Shaping

The following activity illustrates the learning principle of shaping. Students will have the opportunity to shape the behavior of a classmate. This activity is a useful introduction to the material on operant conditioning. It is a vivid activity and has the added benefit of actively involving the entire class. An additional benefit of this activity is that not only does it introduce operant conditioning principles, it also is a nice springboard for material on observational learning.

**DEMONSTRATION:** One student will serve as a volunteer and "operate" on his/her environment. The rest of the class will reinforce desired approximations of an agreed-upon target behavior by clapping until the volunteer performs the target behavior.

**MATERIALS**:
- One extroverted student whose behavior will be shaped

**TIME**: Approximately 20 minutes

**PROCEDURES**:

1. Solicit a volunteer from the class.

2. Explain to the volunteer and the class that the class is going to shape a "desired" behavior. The volunteer will be asked to leave the room while the class decides what behavior will be the target behavior. When the volunteer comes back to the classroom, he/she should "operate" on his/her environment (i.e., engage in different behaviors/actions). The rest of the class will reward the volunteer with clapping when he/she is coming close or approximating the target behavior.

3. Ask for another volunteer from the class to escort your "pigeon" out of the classroom and keep them away while the class decides on a target behavior.

4. While the volunteers are gone, solicit suggestions from the class for a target behavior. Be careful here, it is our experience that the class often can be somewhat sadistic in choosing a target behavior! They will want to get the volunteer to perform some embarrassing behavior (e.g., doing a cartwheel). The suggestion phase is usually pretty funny. Remind the class that he/she who lives by the sword, dies by the sword . . . and that during the semester you will be looking for other volunteers, so they should be careful what they make others do!

5. When choosing a target behavior, make sure that it is: a) a behavior that will be visible to people in the back of the lecture hall; and b) a behavior simple enough to be shaped in about

five minutes or so (e.g., writing on the blackboard, getting up on a chair, dancing the twist, etc.).

6. When the class has agreed upon a target behavior, remind them that they are to reward successive approximations of the desired behavior by clapping.

7. Have your escort bring the volunteer back in and allow the class to shape the behavior.

8. After you have successfully shaped the behavior, thank the volunteer and lead the class in a round of applause for their efforts.

9. Lead the class in a discussion of shaping. Through this discussion, students should get an appreciation for how much easier it is to shape behavior in humans as opposed to animals. (Since humans have language capabilities and can be told what is going on, humans respond well to secondary reinforcers as opposed to animals. Animals become satiated when primary reinforcers are used, etc.) Ask students how they have used shaping in their own lives—e.g., to modify a pet's behavior, to teach a child a procedure, etc. Remind the class of the time involved in shaping—particularly for complex behaviors (e.g., driving a car). Explain how it is often much more efficient to use other learning techniques (like observational learning) to establish a complex behavior.

## Identifying Schedules of Reinforcement

Typically, students have a very difficult time understanding the distinctions among the different schedules of reinforcement found in the operant conditioning section of this chapter (variable ratio, fixed ratio, etc.) The following activity gives students a chance to actively work with this material. In this activity, one student volunteer serves as the "pigeon", and makes an response established by the class (e.g., clapping). The instructor rewards the student with small pieces of candy according to the five primary schedules of reinforcement. The remaining class members must identify which schedule of reinforcement is being used to shape the volunteer's behavior. Not only does this activity work well to clarify the schedules of reinforcement, an instructor also can use the activity as an opportunity to reward other desirable classroom behaviors (e.g., volunteering, participating in class discussions, etc.). Students love this activity and there is nothing like candy to elevate mood!

**DEMONSTRATION:** This activity uses a primary reinforcer (e.g., candy) to illustrate the various schedules of reinforcement.

**MATERIALS**:
- One student to act as your "pigeon"
- A bag of candy like "smarties"
- A couple of blank overhead transparencies

**TIME**: Approximately 30 minutes

**PROCEDURES**:

1. In order for students to get the most of this exercise, it is helpful to either lecture about Skinner's schedules of reinforcement or have students review this material in their text before the exercise.

   Remind students that the ratio schedules require a certain number of correct responses (a fixed number or a variable number) to earn a reward. In the interval schedules the key variable is the span of time (a fixed amount of time or a variable amount of time) that must elapse before a reinforcer is provided. As long as at least one target response occurs during the time period, the organism receives reinforcement.

2. Tell the class that they are going to be detectives—determining which schedule of reinforcement is being used to modify the responses of a target individual.

3. Choose a class volunteer. Establish what response you want the individual to make (e.g., tapping a pencil, clapping—some highly visible behavior).

4. Tell the class and the volunteer that you will be rewarding the individual according to the five standard schedules of reinforcement—continuous, variable interval, variable ratio, fixed interval, fixed ratio. It is often useful to list these on an overhead for the duration of the exercise.

5. Have the class members number their papers from 1–5. They are to observe and note what schedule of reinforcement is being used to train the target person's behavior.

6. Ask the target individual to begin making "responses." Depending on which schedule of reinforcement you are implementing, "reward" the individual with individual pieces of candy. For example,

- **Continuous schedule of reinforcement**: The volunteer receives a piece of candy for each target response. (Note: Be careful here, your volunteer typically figures this out right away and begins clapping like a maniac to get all the candy—you may want to save this schedule for the end or you will run out of candy!)

- **Fixed Ratio**: The volunteer receives a piece of candy for a predetermined number of appropriate responses. For example, every seven claps earns them a piece of candy.

- **Fixed Interval**: The volunteer earns a piece of candy if he/she makes at least one appropriate response during a specified time period. For example, every five seconds (count this in your head or face a clock so as not to be obvious) as long as the volunteer claps once, he/she earns a piece of candy.

- **Variable Interval**: The volunteer earns a piece of candy as long as he/she makes at least one appropriate response during time periods of varying length (e.g., 5 seconds, 10 seconds, 3 seconds).

- **Variable Ratio**: The volunteer earns a piece of candy for a variable number of appropriate responses. For example, give the volunteer a piece of candy for three claps, then for one clap, then for five claps, etc.

7. Confiscate your candy from the volunteer. Thank him/her for being willing to volunteer and very publicly hand him/her a handful of candy.

8. Have class members exchange their sheets and go through each schedule. You may need to re-enact what you did. Have class members score the papers.

9. Ask who correctly identified all of the schedules (usually not many!). Toss these individuals a piece of candy.

10. Engage the class in a discussion of the different schedules. Put each on an overhead and ask students about them. For example, do they lead to a high rate of responding, does the target behavior extinguish quickly or slowly under each schedule? Can they think of a real world example of each schedule? Which schedules did they have the most difficulty identifying (usually the variable schedules—tie this into a discussion of how difficult it is for extinction to occur under the variable schedules)? For each correct response, toss the individual a piece of candy.

11. At the end of the discussion, tell the class that you appreciate their attention/participation in the activity. Toss out the remaining pieces of candy.

Note: Author unknown.

# Chapter 10

# Memory

---

## Recall of a Penny

(Adapted from Nickerson & Adams, 1979)

---

The following activity involves a simple recall task and provides an entertaining way to introduce the topic of forgetting. It is best to do this activity before students have read text material on forgetting, but it will work even if they have read the material.

**DEMONSTRATION:** Students draw both sides of a penny from memory and are scored for accuracy of recall.

**MATERIALS:**
- It is a good idea to bring a few pennies to class when using this activity as proof for skeptics, although in a large class many students will have a penny or two you could use if needed

**TIME:** Approximately 10–15 minutes

**PROCEDURES:**

1. Have students draw about 10 empty circles on a page in their notes. Circles should be about 2 inches in diameter.

2. Instruct students to draw from memory both sides of a U. S. penny. Tell them to include all the pictorial and alphanumeric detail they can. Also tell them they may draw as many versions as they like. Allow them about 10 minutes to complete their drawings.

3. Have students score their drawings according to:
   (a) whether each of the following eight features is present:
   
   Top Side:      Head (Lincoln's Profile)
                        "IN GOD WE TRUST"
                        "LIBERTY"
                        Date
   
   Bottom Side: Building (Lincoln Memorial)
                        "UNITED STATES OF AMERICA"

> "E PLURIBUS UNUM"
> "ONE CENT";

(b) whether each of the above is located on the correct side;

(c) whether each of the above was drawn in the correct position on the circular area. The profile is scored as being in the correct position only if it is drawn as east-facing. Simplify the scoring by using only option a above if you like.

4. With a show of hands compare your class's score with those of Nickerson and Adams. Of the eight critical features the median number recalled and located correctly was three. Not counting the Lincoln head and the Lincoln Memorial, the median number of recalled and correctly located features was one. Only 4 of 20 subjects got as many as half of them correct, and only 1 subject (an active penny collector) accurately recalled and located all eight.

5. Before scoring the activity, you can take it another step. Identify the eight features and ask students to locate them correctly. When Nickerson and Adams gave a group of 20 subjects this task no one located all of the details correctly. Only four were correct on half of them.

6. A third activity involving recognition is to have students number from 1 to 20 on a blank sheet of paper and then read to them the items listed below. Instruct students to write down ("Yes" or "No") whether the feature appears on a penny.

1. The words ONE PENNY
2. The words UNITED STATES OF AMERICA
3. The words ONE NATION UNDER GOD
4. The right side of Washington's face
5. The words ONE CENT
6. The date (year) of mint
7. The great seal
8. The words LINCOLN MEMORIAL
9. The number 1 centered
10. The full face of Lincoln
11. The right side of Lincoln's face
12. A laurel wreath
13. The words MADE IN TAIWAN
14. The Lincoln Memorial
15. The words IN GOD WE TRUST
16. The word LIBERTY
17. The words ANNO DOMINI
18. The word COPPER
19. The words E PLURIBUS UNUM
20. The Statue of Liberty's torch

7. Have students score their responses. (Features 2, 5, 6, 11, 14, 15, 16, and 19 appear on a penny.) Nickerson and Adams' subjects did somewhat better on this activity. The

investigators reported, "The overall probability of a correct response was .85." While you can use your students' better performance on this task to highlight the greater ease of recognition over recall, it is clear that the performance measure is somewhat misleading. As the authors suggest, it may reflect not only the what the subjects remember about a penny but what they infer. Even someone who has never seen a penny might accept some of the features on the basis that they ought to be on a penny (e.g. The United States of America) and reject some others on the grounds that they ought not be there (e.g., Made in Taiwan). (The latter always elicits laughter). Results of these activities demonstrate that the visual details of an object, even a very familiar one, are available from memory only to the degree they are useful in everyday life.

An additional brief memory activity is included here on encoding failure. Much of what we are exposed to, we never notice. You can demonstrate encoding failure by posing the following questions to students suggested by Karl Albrecht.

1. The standard telephone dial has ten numbers, one through nine plus zero. However, it doesn't have all twenty-six letters of the alphabet. Which ones don't appear on the dial? (Ans. "Q" and "Z")

2. What is the color of the top stripe of the American flag? (Ans. Red) The bottom stripe? (Ans. Red) How many red and how many white stripes does it have? (Ans. 7 red and 6 white)

3. Tell students if they have a watch with mechanical hands, to cover the face and try to recall what it looks like. How many numbers does it have? Are they Arabic or Roman numerals— or does it have any numbers at all?

**Related Readings:**

Albrecht, K. (1980). **Brain Power.** Englewood Cliffs, NJ: Prentice-Hall.

Nickerson, R. S., & Adams, M. J. (1979). Long-term memory for a common object. *Cognitive Psychology*, **11**, 287–307.

# Demonstrating the Capacity of Short-Term Memory

The following activity is a class demonstration of the capacity of short-term memory. Our ability to retain and recall new information is limited. As students' psychology texts relate, we can immediately recall roughly seven items of information (Miller, 1956). This activity involves the whole class and can be relied upon to work. It also works as a nice bridge to the various methods we use to try to increase the capacity of our short-term memory (e.g., chunking, attaching meaning to the to-be-remembered information).

**DEMONSTRATION:** Students are read a list of digits out loud, and then asked to recall them in order.

**MATERIALS:** None

**TIME:** Approximately 10–15 minutes

**PROCEDURES:**

1. Ask students to take out a sheet of paper and tell them you will be reading a series of unrelated digits. Their task is to remember the digits in the order in which they are given.

2. Tell students that you will precede each of the digit series with the prompt, "Ready?", and will follow each series with the word, "Recall". This will be the signal for students to write down the series of digits in the order in which they were given.

3. Read at a relatively steady rate—about two digits per second.

4. After you have gone through all the digit strings, have students score their own responses as you re-read the lists.

5. After you have checked students' accuracy rates, ask students by a show of hands, the highest span level at which they got at least one of the series correct. What you should find is that the mean for the class should be slightly above seven.

6. Ask students who did exceptionally well what strategies they used. What students usually report is that they employed some form of chunking (or grouping of digits) as a way of increasing their short-term memory span. Remind students that we do this all the time (e.g., the manner in which we chunk area codes/phone numbers, social security numbers, etc.) Students also report trying to attach some meaning to the digits (similar to a friend's phone number; found patterns in the digit string, etc.). Lead the class in a discussion of different strategies we might employ to try to increase the capacity of our short term memory.

Miller, G. A. (1956). The magical number seven, plus or minus two: Some limits on our capacity for processing information. *Psychology Review*, **63**, 81–97.

| | | | | | | | | | |
|---|---|---|---|---|---|---|---|---|---|
| List 1: | 9 | 7 | 5 | 4 | | | | | |
| List 2: | 6 | 4 | 1 | 9 | | | | | |
| List 3: | 6 | 8 | 2 | 5 | 9 | | | | |
| List 4: | 3 | 7 | 1 | 4 | 8 | | | | |
| List 5: | 91 | 3 | 8 | 2 | 5 | | | | |
| List 6: | 64 | 8 | 3 | 2 | 7 | | | | |
| List 7: | 5 | 9 | 6 | 3 | 8 | 2 | 7* CLASS MEAN | | |
| List 8: | 5 | 3 | 1 | 6 | 8 | 4 | 2 | | |
| List 9: | 8 | 6 | 9 | 5 | 1 | 3 | 7 | 2 | |
| List 10: | 5 | 1 | 7 | 3 | 9 | 8 | 2 | 6 | |
| List 11: | 7 | 1 | 9 | 3 | 8 | 4 | 2 | 7 | 3 |
| List 12: | 1 | 6 | 3 | 8 | 7 | 5 | 9 | 4 | 2 |
| List 13: | 9 | 1 | 5 | 2 | 4 | 3 | 8 | 1 | 6 | 2 |
| List 14: | 1 | 5 | 2 | 8 | 4 | 6 | 7 | 3 | 1 | 8 |

---

# Demonstrating Levels-of-Processing Theory

**(Adapted from Zakrajsek, 1996)**

---

The following brief activity illustrates the levels of processing theory (Craik & Lockhart, 1972) and is based on an activity suggested by Zakrajsek (1996). According to levels of processing theory, recall is enhanced to the extent to which the initial information is processed at a deep rather than a shallow level. In this activity, students are asked to encode a list of words according to one of two sets of instructions. One set of instructions leads to a shallow (non-schematic) processing of information; the other demands deep (schematic) processing. Students are then asked to engage in free recall for the words. Students who are given the latter set of instructions should have a memorial advantage according to levels of processing theory. We use this activity both to illustrate the theory and remind students of how to facilitate memory for course material.

**DEMONSTRATION:** Students are asked to encode words either at a shallow or a deep level (depending on the instructions) and then their memory for words is tested via free recall.

## MATERIALS:
- One sheet of notebook paper per student
- Three prepared overheads (one per set of instructions—see OHTs 10.1, 10.2, 10.3)
- One with the list of to-be-remembered words

**TIME:** Approximately 15 minutes

## PROCEDURES:

1. Tell students that they are going to be taking part in an information processing task and to take out a sheet of paper and number it 1 to 20.

2. Inform students that half the class will be given one set of instructions and the remaining half another set of instructions.

3. Ask half of the class to close their eyes (no cheating!) while the other half reads their set of instructions from (the instructor might, for example, ask students whose surnames begin with A-M to close their eyes, while those with surnames N-Z read their instructions off of the prepared overhead).

4. Once students are clear regarding their instructions, the instructor begins reading the list of words (OHT 10.3) at a 3-second rate.

5. After reading the list, pause and then ask students to write down as many words as they can in any order (free recall test).

6. Allow approximately 2 minutes for recall.

7. Ask students to exchange papers, then place the word list on the overhead and have them check their accuracy.

8. If the activity "worked" (and it usually does), those students who received the "B" set of instructions should have recalled more words as they had the advantage of processing the information at a deeper level than the "A" group. The "A" group processed information at the physical property level while the "B" group assessed the words at a deeper, more meaningful level.

9. Lead the class in a discussion of levels of processing theory. The instructor also might point out other memory phenomena. For example, the instructor might have students check to see if there is evidence of serial position effects in their free recall (i.e., enhanced recall for words at the beginning and end of the list). Students also are expected to demonstrate better memory for those words with which it is easiest to form interactive images (Hyde & Jenkins, 1973). Finally, the instructor might take advantage of this opportunity to remind students how they can facilitate memory for course material—by encoding the information at a deep vs. a shallow level.

**Related Readings:**

Craik, F. I., & Lockhart, R. S. (1972). Levels of processing: A framework for memory research. *Journal of Verbal Behavior*, **11**, 671–684.

Hyde, T. S. & Jenkins, J. J. (1973). Recall of words as a function of semantic, graphic, and syntactic orienting tasks. *Journal of Verbal Learning and Verbal Behavior*, **12**, 471–480.

Zakrajsek, T. (1996). Exploring levels of processing theory. In **Instructor's Manual to accompany Feldman Understanding Psychology** (4th Ed.). New York: McGraw-Hill, Inc.

OHT 10.1

# INSTRUCTIONS—"A"

**YOU WILL BE READ A LIST OF WORDS.**

**YOUR JOB IS TO EITHER COUNT OR ESTIMATE THE NUMBER OF VOWELS PRESENT IN EACH WORD.**

**PLEASE JOT DOWN YOUR VOWEL ESTIMATE AFTER EACH WORD IS READ.**

# INSTRUCTIONS—"B"

YOU WILL BE READ A LIST OF WORDS.

YOUR JOB IS TO RATE EACH WORD ON A 5 POINT SCALE OF IMPORTANCE IF YOU WERE STRANDED ON A SOUTH SEA ISLAND.
(5 = VERY IMPORTANT)

PLEASE JOT DOWN YOUR RATING AFTER EACH WORD IS READ.

# WORD LIST

1. UMBRELLA
2. GASOLINE
3. ORCHESTRA
4. YACHT
5. HAMMER
6. DIAMOND
7. UNIVERSITY
8. MACARONI
9. EYEGLASSES
10. GARDEN
11. UNDERWEAR
12. NEWSPAPER
13. ALCOHOL
14. BOTTLE
15. MICROSCOPE
16. CAMOUFLAGE
17. SULFUR
18. RESTAURANT
19. INSECT
20. LEMONADE

# The Fallibility of Eyewitness Testimony

The following activity is a very vivid (and memorable!) demonstration of the fallibility of eyewitness testimony. The instructor arranges for a confederate to burst into the classroom and steal something (e.g., instructor's briefcase) during lecture. After the "crime" has been committed, students are asked to provide eyewitness testimony. Students love this activity. It serves as a useful tool to discuss a) eyewitness testimony research, b) the three major processes of memory (encoding, storage and retrieval) and c) bystander intervention. It is best to do this activity before students have read text material on eye-witness testimony.

**DEMONSTRATION:** Students are eyewitnesses to a "crime" committed in class and have the opportunity to test the accuracy of their memory for the perpetrator.

**MATERIALS:**
- One extroverted confederate
- An overhead transparency (OHT 10.4)
- One sheet of notebook paper per student

**TIME:** Approximately 20–30 minutes

**PROCEDURES:**

1. Before beginning the discussion of eyewitness testimony, arrange for a confederate to be your thief . . . they can be a member of the class as long as they dress to disguise themselves.

2. Have your confederate dress so that class members have plenty of items to remember (e.g. many layers of clothing, jewelry, etc.). Also, have the confederate come into the classroom brandishing something which may be perceived as a weapon (e.g., a pair of scissors, a wrench, lead pipe, etc.) Be careful here, you don't want the confederate carrying something that could be dangerous in case a class member decided to heroically intervene to stop the intruder! We also ask the confederate to shout something so that the class has even more to remember.

3. Begin class. When you are in the middle of lecture, the thief should burst into the room shouting, steal some article from the front of the classroom, and make his/her escape.

4. The class will stop dead . . . there will be some shock and rustling. After this has dissipated, tell the class that they have just witnessed a crime and they will need to provide usable information to the police.

5. Have each student take out a piece of paper to jot down his/her information.

6. On a prepared overhead (see **OHT 10.4**), prime the class' memory for the event/assailant with various questions (e.g. What was the person's gender, race, height, weight, hair color, clothing, color of clothing, etc.; What was the crime that was committed?; Did the person say anything? What? Was there anything else that was distinctive about the individual? If so, what?, etc.). Ask students to estimate how accurate their eyewitness testimony is on a scale from 0 to 100%. Poll the class using a show of hands on how accurate they think themselves to be.

7. After students have provided their written eyewitness testimony, ask your thief to come back in and allow the class to check on their accuracy. Usually students are quite inaccurate, especially those sitting in the back of the room. At this point, there is usually a lot of giggling and sheepish discussion among students. Ask the class to give your "thief" a round of applause for his/her acting ability.

8. Lead the class in a discussion of some of the issues involved in eyewitness testimony. Specifically, remind students of how they were in an almost idyllic position to provide accurate eyewitness testimony when one considers the three processes involved in memory: encoding, storage and retrieval. In terms of encoding the information, students had a number of advantages—they were sitting in a well-lit location, with very little to distract them. Moreover, they hopefully were already conditioned to pay attention to the front of the classroom! They probably did not believe themselves to be in any danger, etc. Considering the storage process of memory, you elicited the to-be-remembered information fairly quickly. In terms of retrieval, primes were given to help them retrieve the information but the primes were not designed to confuse or obfuscate. During this discussion, bring in Elizabeth Loftus' research on the reconstructive nature of eyewitness testimony, the weapons-focus effect (i.e., the tendency for witnesses to focus on the weapon during the crime, rendering facial identification less accurate), cross-racial identification bias (our tendency to show more accuracy when identifying someone from our own racial category), etc.

9. Depending on time parameters, you also might lead the class in a discussion of some of the current controversies in the area of eyewitness testimony (e.g., the authenticity of repressed memories, the ability of children to provide accurate eyewitness testimony, etc.). The instructor also might ask the class if anyone has ever been brought to court to provide eyewitness testimony (usually in a large class, someone has). Finally, depending on what transpires during the incident, the instructor also might discuss bystander intervention issues. A note here—be prepared—every once in a while, we have a student who tries to intervene (may start yelling at the thief, may try running after him/her). This incident occurs so quickly that this rarely occurs,

but if it does be sure that both parties are kept "safe." Also, keep in mind that the person who intervenes may end up feeling foolish. Usually, we counteract this by publicly thanking the person for their courage and leading the class in a round of applause for your "hero."

10. Optional: We will often use this as in-class extra credit/attendance check by collecting students' papers.

**Related Reading:**

Loftus, E. F., & Palmer, J. C. (1974). Reconstruction of automobile destruction: An example of the interaction between language and memory. *Journal of Verbal Learning and Verbal Behavior*, **13**, 585–589.

**What was the person's:**

      **Gender**
      **Race**
      **Height**
      **Weight**
      **Hair color**
      **Clothing**
      **Color of clothing**

**What was the crime that was committed?**

**Did the person say anything?**

**What?**

**Was there anything else that was distinctive about the individual? If so, what was it?**

# Chapter 11

# Cognition and Language

The following brief activity illustrates some of the common cognitive heuristics that we use when we make judgments. In this block of material, heuristics are often described as rules-of-thumb, which are quick and easy but which frequently cause us to make errors in judgment. In this activity, students are exposed to the representativeness heuristic, which hinges upon our failure to consider base-rate information (e.g., numerical base rates or prior probabilities) when making judgments. Students also are exposed to the availability heuristic, which involves our tendency to judge the probability of an event by the ease in which prior occurrences come to mind. The beauty of this mini-activity is that it is very reliable, seldom failing. It is based on some of the classic research on cognitive heuristics by Kahneman & Tversky (1973).

**DEMONSTRATION:** The instructor reads a passage and asks students to make probability judgments.

**MATERIALS**: None

**TIME**: Approximately 5 minutes

**PROCEDURES**:

1.  Ask students to listen to the following description carefully:

    Mary is a quiet individual, reserved and shy. Neat and orderly, Mary's hobbies include reading, crafting, and listening to classical music.

    **Is Mary more likely to be:**
    **a.  an airline pilot?**
    **b.  a salesperson?**
    **c.  a librarian?**

2. Ask the class for a show of hands to see who endorsed each option. After getting a show of hands, ask class members why they endorsed each particular option. Typically, about three-quarters of the class endorses option "c." When asked why they believe Mary to be a librarian, class members will usually suggest that Mary's characteristics seem most consistent with those we associate with a librarian (e.g., quiet and neat).

3. Ask the class, in relative terms are there more people who work as airline pilots, salespeople, or librarians? Rather sheepishly the class will respond "salespeople".

4. Define the availability heuristic for students. Explain that the description of Mary seems more consistent with our stereotyped image of a librarian than an airline pilot or a salesperson. We generally rely on this information rather than utilizing probability information. Based on pure numerical probabilities, students should have responded "salesperson." There are many more salespeople than librarians.

5. Have the class explore how the representativeness heuristic can lead to potential problems in person perception. For example, it can readily be seen how this heuristic can form the basis for stereotyping individuals. Ask the class if they can think of other situations when we do not take advantage of numerical base-rate information when making decisions (e.g., playing the lottery, jumping into a weight loss program based on a few select influential testimonials rather than looking at what people lose on average, etc.).

6. Next, ask the class the following:

**Is the letter "r" more likely to appear as the first letter in a word or as the third letter?**

7. Get a show of hands from the class. Again, the majority of the class will usually think more words begin with the letter "r" than have "r" appear as the third letter.

8. The correct answer, of course is the latter option. We tend to choose the first option based on another cognitive heuristic—the availability heuristic. Because when we think about this problem it is easier for us to generate words where "r" is the first letter (i.e., such words are more readily available to us in memory) and we draw an erroneous conclusion. Help the class see the connection between the availability heuristic and our tendency to overestimate the probability of events such as tornadoes, plane accidents, not guilty by-reason-of-insanity verdicts. These events tend to receive a lot of hype in the media and thus are readily available in our memory. When one examines the actual incident rates, they are relatively infrequently occurring events.

**Related Reading:**

Kahneman, D., & Tversky, A. (1973). On the psychology of prediction. *Psychological Review*, **80**, 237–251.

## Functional Fixedness and Problem Solving

The following brief activity illustrates the concept of functional fixedness and divergent vs. convergent thinking in problem-solving. We use this when we begin the material on problem-solving. The activity really gets students involved and tends to promote a lot of discussion. This activity serves to loosen students up.

**DEMONSTRATION:** Students generate as many possible uses for an item as possible in a five minute period.

**MATERIALS:**
■  Some object (e.g., stack of post-it notes, brick, clothes hanger, Kleenex)

**TIME:** Approximately 5 minutes

**PROCEDURES:**

1. At the beginning of the lecture on problem-solving, tell students class members are going to test their creativity. Explain that one of the major barriers to creative problem solving is thinking about an issue in the same routinized ways: an unwillingness to step outside of the lines when approaching a problem.

2. Have students generate ideas for how to use the object in novel ways.

3. List the ideas generated on an overhead transparency. (An alternative to this is to have students do this in small groups. The group that generates the most items within the given time period can be awarded extra credit points.)

4. Lead the class in a discussion of how it is useful to try to get out of our own mental rut when thinking about a problem. Define functional fixedness and get some examples from the class on how they have solved problems by using an object in a novel way (e.g., using a clothes hanger to hold up a dragging muffler). Describe how we often develop our own "learning sets" (the tendency to solve all problems using

the same strategy). Explain how these strategies develop over time and are maintained by us because they typically have lead to successful outcomes. Provide students with an example (e.g., how they typically study for an exam). Have them explore how their typical studying strategy (e.g., concentrating on the notes) may have served them well across exams in one particular class, but ill-serves them in another class in which the instructor emphasizes material from the textbook.

# The Importance of Expectancies in Understanding Languages

**(Adapted from Diekhoff, 1987)**

The following brief activity demonstrates how our perception of language is heavily impacted by what we expect to hear or read. The activity is based on Diekhoff (1987) and can be used with the entire class. Given our experience with both written and spoken language, we expect language to conform to certain rules of grammar, spelling, and semantics. These rules cause us to expect certain word and letter strings over others. The relative ease and accuracy of our perceptions of words/sentences is influenced by the degree to which they are consistent with our expectancies (Miller & Isard, 1963). Students are presented with two stimuli in which language rules are not followed and then are asked to describe what they perceived. Students usually distort their perceptions in a manner that is more congruent with the typical rules of language. This activity allows students to see how perception is a constructive process.

**DEMONSTRATION:** Students are presented with two stimuli (one visual and one verbal) in which language rules are not followed. Students are asked to describe in writing what they saw/heard.

**MATERIALS:**
- One sheet of notebook paper per student
- Two prepared overheads (see OHT 11.1 and 11.2)

**TIME**: Approximately 15 minutes

**PROCEDURES**:

1. Tell students that you are going to show them a short message very briefly and that they are to write down what they see.

2. Show students the stimulus for no more than three seconds.

3. After students have written down what they saw, with a show of hands, ask students how many saw, "Flowers bloom in the spring." Typically, approximately two-thirds of the class will respond affirmatively.

4. Show students the stimulus again and point out the error.

5. Next, tell students that you will read several sentences slowly but only once. Their task is to write down each sentence verbatim as it is read.

6. Read the prepared sentences at a speed that ensures students can transcribe the grammatical/meaningful sentences accurately. Wait a second or two and then ask students to write down the sentence that they heard.

    a. The dog looked warily over its shoulder and then gobbled down the hot dog.
    (14 words)
    (Grammatical and Meaningful)

    b. The door ate the sky loudly, but would not drop the ocean.
    (12 words)
    (Grammatical but Meaningless)

    c. Door ocean the quickly sky over drop shoulder the not warily and.
    (12 words)
    (Non-grammatical and Meaningless)

7. Have students exchange papers and count the number of words copied correctly from each sentence (using **OHT 11.2**).

8. With a show of hands, ask how many words students were able to transcribe accurately per sentence.

9. Have the class compare the number of accurately copied words for each of the three types of sentences. What you should find is that accuracy is highest for the sentence that is both grammatically accurate and meaningful. The sentence that is non-grammatical and meaningless should register the lowest accuracy rates.

10. Lead the class in a discussion of these two exercises. What general language principle do both illustrate (i.e., that our perception of language conforms to grammar-based expectancies)? In the first exercise, the second "the" is generally not perceived since

it violates our rules of grammar that prohibit a word's occurrence twice in sequence. In the second exercise, accuracy rates tend to be highest for the first sentence since neither the rules of grammar nor those of semantics are violated. Non-grammatical and meaningless sentences (sentence 3) are the most difficult for us to perceive accurately since both rules of grammar and semantics are violated (i.e., none of our language expectancies hold).

11. Although these activities relate most obviously to language, the instructor also might want to discuss how one's expectancies influence other situations (e.g., a first date, an instructor's/students initial perceptions of a class, eyewitness testimony, an experimenter's perceptions regarding the likely outcome of an experiment, etc.). Engage the class in a discussion of how our expectancies can color what we come away with in different situations. Ask students why we reliably show these expectancies? How does holding such expectancies help/hinder perception (i.e., accuracy vs. cognitive effort tradeoffs).

**Related Readings:**

Diekhoff, G. M. (1987). The role of expectancies in the perception of language. In **Activities Handbook for the teaching of psychology** (Vol. 2). Washington, DC: American Psychological Association.

Miller, G. A., & Isard, S. (1963). Some perceptual consequences of linguistic rules. *Journal of Verbal Learning and Verbal Behavior*, **2**, 217–228.

FLOWERS BLOOM

IN THE SPRING.

1. **THE DOG LOOKED WARILY OVER ITS SHOULDER AND THEN GOBBLED DOWN THE HOT DOG.**

2. **THE DOOR ATE THE SKY LOUDLY, BUT WOULD NOT DROP THE OCEAN.**

3. **DOOR OCEAN THE QUICKLY SKY OVER DROP SHOULD THE NOT WARILY AND.**

# Chapter 12

## Intelligence

## What Does an Intelligence

## Test Measure?

The following activity may be used to introduce the topic of intelligence, as well as illustrate the difficulties associated with defining and measuring this construct. This activity also should help students gain an appreciation of reliability and validity. Finally, the activity may be used to illustrate employment testing in Industrial/Organizational Psychology.

**DEMONSTRATION:** Students take an actual employment test designed in the 1930s to measure intelligence.

**MATERIALS:**
- One piece of notebook paper per student
- Overhead Transparency (see OHT 12.1)

**TIME:** Approximately 10 minutes

**PROCEDURES:**

1. Before discussing the topic of Intelligence, tell students that you are going to begin the class by giving them a short intelligence test. Inform them that this particular test was used in employment testing to measure intelligence.

2. Ask students to use a piece of notebook paper to respond to the following 14 multiple choice questions—which you will read out loud and show on an overhead transparency (see **OHT 12.1**). If they need for you to repeat the question or alternatives, they should raise their hands. Each question has one correct answer. Specific questions follow the explanation of this exercise.

3. After presenting students with the 14 questions, tell them that you will read the correct answer so that they can score their own tests. After students have scored their exams, ask for a show of hands of those who had all 14 answers correct. Usually 2–3 students will respond. Tell these students that had they taken this test in 1939 and scored this well, they would have been top job candidates for a position of firefighter in a large metropolitan area. Explain to students that this test was actually used to measure intelligence for a position of firefighter.

4. Now, ask students if they think this is a good measure of intelligence, and if not, why not. They typically will come up with the following responses—the answers to some of the questions don't really have one correct answer (they are just opinions), some of the questions rely on experience as opposed to intelligence, some of the questions have nothing to do with intelligence, some of the questions are biased, etc. Ask them if they think it was a good selection test to use for firefighters. Obviously, the test does not seem to be job-related.

5. Use this example to further illustrate and discuss the difficulty of creating good measures of intelligence (e.g., importance of culture-fairness, reliability, validity). Discuss potential problems created by using intelligence tests in employment selection decisions, and in academic settings. What are the dangers associated with intelligence testing?

In the 1930s and 1940s, the following test was used by a large city in its selection of firefighters. The test was designed to be a measure of intelligence, which was believed to be positively correlated with successful job performance. Correct answers are indicated below:

1) e; 2) b; 3) c; 4) c; 5) d; 6) d; 7) a; 8) c; 9) e;
10) d; 11) e ; 12) a; 13) c; 14) a

## Test Questions from the Entrance Examinations For The Position of Firefighter (1939)

1. Why is it so hard to breathe on a high mountain?
   a. the wind blows your breath away
   b. it is always cold
   c. you are exhausted
   d. you are too close to the sun
   e. the air is rare

2. Which was the original mail order house?
   a. Smith & Wesson
   b. Sears, Roebuck & Co.
   c. L. C. Smith
   d. Hart, Shaffner, & Marx
   e. National Biscuit Company

3. Why do men seek the presidency?
   a. they can live in Washington
   b. they can travel
   c. they become famous
   d. they become rich
   e. they can make speeches

4. What do the letters H.R.H. stand for?
   a. an atomic weight
   b. a chemistry formula
   c. a person
   d. a ship
   e. a country

5. **Why are airplanes used for mail service?**
   a. they cannot be robbed
   b. they are not stopped by storms
   c. they are cheaper than trains
   d. they are very swift

6. **Why should the constitution be respected?**
   a. it has often been amended
   b. it is the best constitution
   c. it is disloyal to criticize it
   d. it is the highest law of the land
   e. it was made by our fathers

7. **Which man lived the longest time ago?**
   a. Marquette
   b. Washington
   c. Jackson
   d. Lafayette
   e. Sheridan

8. **Why is a train harder to stop than an automobile?**
   a. it is longer
   b. it takes more people to stop it
   c. it is heavier
   d. it runs on tracks

9. **Why is electricity found in many rural districts where there is no sewer system?**
   a. electricity is more necessary to health
   b. it is wanted by the farmers
   c. it is less expensive to install
   d. it never gets out of order
   e. it causes fewer fires than kerosene lamps

10. For what is "Good Housekeeping" a name?
    a. vacuum cleaner
    b. washing machine
    c. floor polish
    d. magazine
    e. novel

11. Why do people buy Liberty Bonds?
    a. they pay a high rate of interest
    b. they have lots of coupons
    c. they are long time bonds
    d. they can be registered
    e. they are secured by the government

12. Why should criminals be locked up?
    a. to protect society
    b. to make them work
    c. to get even with them
    d. to punish them
    e. to scare them

13. What is the most useful thing doctors can do?
    a. hold consultations
    b. cheer up patients
    c. prevent disease
    d. run hospitals
    e. give medicine

14. Who wrote the Koran?
    a. Mohammed
    b. Buddha
    c. Confucius
    d. Moses
    e. Mrs. Eddy

## A Demonstration of the Impact of Teacher Expectations on Intellectual Performance

The following activity is intended to help students understand how environmental factors (e.g., teacher expectations) can impact a person's intellectual achievement. The activity is based on Rosenthal & Jacobson's classic 1968 study in which teachers were informed that one group of students (the late bloomer) group would perform exceptionally well over the next year. In reality, this group possessed the same ability as the other group and had been chosen at random. At the end of the school year, the late bloomer group were reported to have out-performed the rest of the class. Results were interpreted as being due to differential teacher expectations and subsequent behavior directed toward the late bloomer group. While students may in the abstract understand the "nurture" side of the nature/nurture argument as it relates to achievement, the following activity really brings it home. Over a two day period, class members are either praised or derogated for their conduct in class (i.e., the instructor creates a warm/chilly classroom environment). While this activity may arouse some hostility on the part of students, after they have been debriefed, they acknowledge that it was a powerful experience. Moreover, it can be used to bring in a number of other lecture topics (e.g., self-fulfilling prophecy; confirmatory hypothesis testing in employment interviews; prejudice/discrimination, educational interventions, etc.).

**DEMONSTRATION**: Over two class periods, the instructor encourages the intellectual strivings of one group of students while actively discouraging the same in another group of students. After the second class, students process what went on and how this relates to intellectual achievement.

**MATERIALS**: None

**TIME**: Two class periods

**PROCEDURES**:

1. (Note: this activity usually works best if used a couple of class periods before beginning the material on intelligence.) Before class, the instructor determines some basis for grouping students. We often use gender since it is easiest and leads to some interesting discussions afterward. The "down" group will bear the brunt of a chilly classroom climate for the first lecture period.

2. During the first lecture period, the instructor should be sure to ask a number of questions, solicit examples from the class, etc. When members of the "down" group raise or respond to questions, the instructor should respond negatively. The instructor should make comments along these lines, "That doesn't make any sense; Please listen again to my question; No, that is incorrect." Nonverbals should be consistent as well (e.g., no eye contact, walking away, bored facial expression, etc.). Responses from your "intelligent for the day" group should be treated in the opposite matter (e.g. "terrific example! Great insight! What a well-reasoned answer," etc.). Nonverbals should include extensive eye contact, smiling, nodding, etc.

3. Over the span of the class, you should notice that the class participation of your "down" group will start to dissipate while that of your "up" group increases.

4. During the next class period, switch groups and engage in the same behaviors.

5. At the end of the class period, ask students if they noticed anything going on in class. Usually somebody is able to identify the pattern. Once the pattern has been pointed out to the class, ask class members how they felt on each day. Ask them if they noticed anything in terms of class participation, how much they enjoyed being in class, etc.

6. Lead the class in a discussion of how aspects of the environment (e.g., resources available for learning; teacher expectations; parental expectations, etc.) can influence student achievement. The instructor also can tie this into some of the research on chilly climate for females, which suggests that females are treated differently in the classroom compared to males (not asked challenging questions; posed questions that call for simple responses, etc.). Ask the class what an instructor can do to ensure that he/she is not creating a chilly climate for any students. Education majors typically have a lot to say regarding possible interventions. It is interesting to note that some research indicates that even teachers who are aware of the "chilly climate" effect for female students nevertheless still fall prey to it.

7. During the debriefing phase, the instructor should be sure to impress upon students that any verbals/nonverbals over the last couple of days had absolutely nothing to do with the quality of their class participation. The instructor may (if appropriate) want to suggest that it was awfully difficult not to reinforce some of the really good answers that the "down" group gave. It also is important to keep in mind that this activity may lead to some student resistance (from your "down" groups). In order for the activity to work, it is important that the instructor stick to the script, as difficult as it may be to do so.

**Related Reading:**

Rosenthal, R., & Jacobson, L. (1968). Pygmalion in the classroom. New York: Holt, Rinehart & Winston.

# The Case for Multiple Intelligences

The following activity introduces the notion of multiple intelligence (Gardner, 1983). Students have an opportunity to become more personally involved in the lecture material by relating different forms of intelligence to people they personally know and to themselves.

**DEMONSTRATION:** For each type of intelligence, students write down the name of a person who exemplifies a high amount of intelligence. In addition, students rate their own intellectual abilities for each type.

**MATERIALS**:
- One piece of notebook paper per student
- Overhead transparency (see OHT 12.2)

**TIME**: Approximately 10 minutes

**PROCEDURES**:

1. After introducing Gardner's notion of multiple intelligence, display the overhead transparency listing the six types of intelligence. These include: linguistic, logical-mathematical, spatial, musical, bodily-kinesthetic, and personal. Give students a brief description of each type of intelligence. The first three are often included in standard measures of intelligence and most students are familiar with these terms. In addition, most students will understand the concept of "musical intelligence." Bodily-kinesthetic reflects the ability to learn and perform complex body movements (e.g., athletes). Personal intelligence reflects the ability to understand others and oneself. This form of intelligence is sometimes referred to as "emotional intelligence."

2. Ask students to copy the list on the overhead (see **OHT 12.2**). After each form of intelligence, they should write down the name of a person they know who shows a high amount of the particular form of intelligence. In addition ask them to indicate if they, themselves, are high, medium, or low on this dimension.
3. Discuss the concept of multiple versus general intelligence. Do students believe that all of the above qualities are really forms of intelligence? Why or why not? Discuss Gardner's notion of independent intelligences. Do students know any people who are high in all forms of intelligence? Why is it valuable to look at intelligence from the

perspective of multiple intelligence? How do divergent forms of intelligence help us to survive?

**Related Reading:**

Gardner, H. (1983). Frames of mind: The theory of multiple intelligences. New York: Basic Books.

# Gardner's Six Types of Intelligence

**Linguistic**

**Logical-mathematical**

**Spatial**

**Musical**

**Bodily-kinesthetic**

**Personal**

# Chapter 13

## Motivation and Emotion

```
Something You've Always
Wanted to Know About Sex
but Were Afraid to Ask
```

Students usually enjoy discussions about sexual motivation and behavior. However, large class sizes inhibit most students from taking an active role. The following activity gives all students an opportunity to become more personally involved in the lecture material by submitting anonymous questions they have about sexual motivation and behavior. The responses used to answer these questions can be organized in ways to illustrate several important findings in the area of sexual motivation and behavior.

**DEMONSTRATION:** One class period before the motivation lecture, students are asked to submit one question about sexual motivation or behavior. These questions form the basis for the subsequent lecture on motivation.

**MATERIALS:**
- One piece of notebook paper per student

**TIME:** Approximately 5 minutes for students to write and submit a question

**PROCEDURES:**

1. One class period before lecturing on sexual motivation and behavior, introduce the exercise to the students. Tell them that the next lecture will be on sexual motivation and that you would like to try to answer questions they have about sexual behavior. At this point, relay that many people have questions about sexual motivation and behavior—but they are often inhibited and afraid to ask. Ask students to take out a piece of notebook paper and write down a question they have about sexual behavior. (Assure them that their questions are confidential and they will not be personally identified.) Then have the students turn in their questions.

2. Sort these questions into common themes. Teaching assistants usually find helping with this task to be a fun activity as well.

3. Prepare your lecture around these major themes. Typically, questions fall into categories that allow you to talk about: how sexual motivation is different from other kinds of motivation (e.g., examples of other biological and social motives); how humans' sexual behavior differs from that of other animals; the relative role of biology versus the brain; how males and females differ; the sexual response cycle and orgasm; the effects of various factors—such as age, marital status, alcohol and drugs, etc.; and sexual dysfunctions and remedies.

4. When delivering the lecture, begin each topic by reading several relevant questions that you will be trying to answer. Students enjoy the personalized approach. (Note: You might point out to students that they are uncomfortable with this topic as evidenced by the fact that many of them folded their question sheet several times before handing it in. They appeared to be afraid someone would see what they wrote. This fits well with a discussion of the semi-restrictiveness in attitudes towards sexuality in our culture compared to other less restrictive cultures).

## The Universality of Emotions: Testing Ekman's Theory

The following activity illustrates Paul Ekman's theory which postulates that emotional expression is a universal phenomenon. Ekman (1994) suggests that there are six primary emotions (happiness, sadness, disgust, fear, surprise, and anger). He argues that people from different countries/cultures show an amazing consistency in both their ability to decipher these emotions and display them (i.e., that emotional expression is innate, unlearned). Student volunteers are asked to display "universal" emotions; the remainder of the class must determine what emotional state the volunteers are experiencing. The activity then becomes a springboard for other issues relating to emotional expression (e.g., the facial feedback hypothesis, the relative utility of being able to read others' emotions, cultural influences on emotional expression indicated by display rules, etc.).

**DEMONSTRATION:** Five students volunteer to display certain emotions. The rest of the class must determine what emotion each volunteer is experiencing.

**MATERIALS**:

- Six extroverted students
- Six notecards
- One page of notebook paper per student

**TIME**: Approximately 20 minutes

**PROCEDURES**:

1. On each of six notecards, write some scenario designed to engender one of Ekman's six primary emotions. The notecard is to get your volunteer in the "mood".

   For example,

   a. You open the door and the Prize Patrol is outside. You have just won the $20 million dollar Publisher's Clearinghouse Award. You are **HAPPY.**

   b. You go to the cafeteria for lunch and are about to bite into your salad when you see a huge hard-backed cockroach crawling in the lettuce . . . antennae waving. You are **DISGUSTED.**

   c. You find out that your pet cat of 19 years was run over by a Mac truck. You are **SAD.**

   d. You find out that your girlfriend/boyfriend is sleeping with your best friend. You are **ANGRY.**

   e. You are walking across campus at 2 A.M. You hear footsteps and heavy breathing right behind you. You are **AFRAID.**

   f. You find out that you and your instructor are long lost cousins. You are **SURPRISED.** (Hopefully not disgusted or saddened!).

2. Before class, solicit six students to be the target individuals. Explain the purpose of demonstration and give them their notecards.

3. Explain to the rest of the class that it is their job to determine what emotion each of the volunteers is experiencing. Have the class members number their papers from 1– 6. Class members should indicate what emotion each volunteer is experiencing.

4. Ask the volunteers to come up front. Have each display the emotional state that corresponds to their notecard. Warn the volunteers that they are to use only their facial expressions to get across their emotion.

5. After going through the six volunteers, have students exchange their papers with someone nearby for scoring. Poll the class with a show of hands on what emotion they thought each volunteer was experiencing. Then have each volunteer read their scenario.

6. Thank your volunteers and have the class give them a hand for their "acting".

7. Lead the class in a discussion of Ekman's research and related research on the universality of the display and interpretation of emotions. Point out that many (including Ekman & Charles Darwin) believe that it was beneficial from a survival standpoint to be able to both register and decipher emotions. Ask the class why this might be important (e.g. being able to predict when your boyfriend/girlfriend is angry, in the mood, knowing when to hit up your boss for a raise, avoiding dangerous situations, being responsive to a newborn, etc.). Incidentally, some research suggests that it may be difficult for us to discriminate between surprise and fear. Ask the class why this may be (the standard explanation is that these emotions often occur simultaneously in real life and are engendered by the same sorts of situations).

**Related Readings:**

Darwin, C. (1972/1965). **The expression of the emotions in man and animals.** Chicago: University of Chicago Press.

Ekman, P. (1994). Strong evidence for universals in facial expressions: A reply to Russel's mistaken critique. *Psychological Bulletin*, **115**, 268–287.

Ekman, P., & Friesen, W. (1971). Constants across cultures in the face and emotion. *Journal of Personality and Social Psychology*, **17**, 124–129.

## The Facial Feedback Hypothesis

**(Adapted from Bolt and Myers, 1983)**

This activity illustrates how our facial expressions produce sensory feedback, which in turn helps our brain interpret subjective, emotional reactions. It is based on the facial feedback hypothesis (Izard, 1977). Students find this activity fun and involving. It is a modification of an exercise suggested by Bolt and Myers (1983).

**DEMONSTRATION:** Students are asked to display various facial expressions and monitor their emotional reactions.

**MATERIALS:** None

**TIME:** Approximately 5 minutes.

**PROCEDURES:**

1. After lecturing on emotion and summarizing research on the facial feedback hypothesis, tell students that you would like them to test the hypothesis for themselves.

2. First ask students to make a sad face. Have them furrow their brows, turn down the corners of their mouths, etc. Ask them to subjectively rate how they feel and write this down in their notebooks. Then ask them to make a happy face. Have them turn up the corners of their mouths, raise their eyes, etc. Again, have them record how they feel. Ask them if their mood improved.

3. Ask students if they can alter their moods. Do they have control over how they feel? What implications does the facial feedback hypothesis have for our day-to-day lives?

**Related Readings:**

Bolt, M. and Myers, D. G. (1983). **Teacher's Resource and Test Manual to Accompany Social Psychology**, New York: McGraw-Hill, Inc.

Izard, C. E. (1977). **Human emotions.** New York: Plenum.

---

## Detecting Deception in Others

---

The following activity illustrates how difficult it is to use verbal and nonverbal cues to detect deception in others. Many students tend to think they are very adept at detecting deception, but usually the class fares quite poorly in determining who is lying and who is not. Students tend to enjoy this activity since detecting others' deception is something they deal with on a regular basis—e.g., an instructor who must determine if a student is giving a bogus excuse for missing an exam, an individual who must assess whether their girlfriend or boyfriend is telling the truth about an event, a manager who must determine if an interviewee is being truthful about his/her credentials, etc.

**DEMONSTRATION:** Five students volunteer to either lie or tell the truth about their lives. The rest of the class must determine who is lying and who is not.

**MATERIALS:**
- Five extroverted students to describe something about their lives
- Five notecards
- One piece of notebook paper per student

**TIME:** Approximately 20 minutes

**PROCEDURES:**

1. On each of five notecards, write the following:

   In a few sentences or so, I would like you to describe for the class

   - who makes up your family
   - why you are taking this class
   - the time you met someone famous
   - the thing you are most afraid of
   - your political party and who you voted for in the last presidential election.

   Please (*tell the truth/lie*).

2. Before class, solicit five students to be the target individuals. Explain the purpose of demonstration and give them a few minutes to think about what they will say.

3. Explain to the rest of the class that it is their job to determine who is lying and who is telling the truth. Have the class members number their papers from 1–5. Class members should indicate whether each individual was telling the truth or lying and what cues they used to make their decisions.

4. In order, ask each student a question that corresponds with their notecard. For example, "What political party do you identify with and whom did you vote for in the last presidential election?"

5. After going through the five questions, have students exchange their papers with someone nearby for scoring. Go back through the questions and poll the class about whether each individual was lying or telling the truth. Ask the target individuals whether they lied or did not lie.

6. Thank your target individuals and have the class give them a hand for their "acting".

7. Lead the class in a discussion of the verbal and nonverbal cues they think are associated with deception. Relay some of the research on this subject. For example, research by Greene, O'Hair, Cody, and Yen (1985) suggests that there are reliable

cues to deception including: an increase in body shifts, foot movements, errors in speech, voice pitch, and gestures to the face; and a decrease in eye contact and hand gestures. Ekman (1985) suggests that when trying to determine who is lying, we tend to focus on the wrong cues. Most people focus on the face as the primary cue to use when seeking to uncover deception. However, Ekman's research indicates that facial cues are often the least diagnostic since practiced liars tend to become proficient at schooling their facial cues.

**Related Readings:**

Ekman, P. (1985). **Telling lies: Cues to deceit in the marketplace, politics and marriage.** New York: Norton.

Greene, J. O., O'Hair, H.D., Cody, M. J., & Yen, C. (1985). Planning and control of behavior during deception. *Human Communication Research*, **11**, 335–364.

# Chapter 14

# Child and Adolescent Development

```
Exploring How We Change
Through the Lifespan
```

Students can actively explore various developmental stages by reflecting on memories of significant personal events in childhood and adolescence, and important events and accomplishments experienced or anticipated during young, middle, and late adulthood. The following activity can be used to introduce the topic of developmental psychology by focusing on ways people develop and change (e.g., physical development, problem solving, language, personality, morals, social interests, etc.). In later discussions, it can be used to illustrate Erikson's theory of life span development. It also may be used to discuss stereotypes of aging or gender differences.

**DEMONSTRATION:** Students provide written examples of important events, memories, and accomplishments associated with various periods of their own development.

**MATERIALS:**
- One piece of notebook paper per student
- Overhead transparency (see OHT 14.1)

**TIME:** Approximately 15 minutes

**PROCEDURES:**

1. Begin the class by asking students to take out a piece of notebook paper and label it according to the age categories presented on the overhead projector (see **OHT 14.1**). Tell them that you want them to think about their own development during each of these time periods. Then tell the students that they will have 15 minutes to jot down important events, memories, and accomplishments they experienced or anticipate experiencing during each of the eight periods. Ask them to list those things that were most important to them at various times.

2. Acknowledge that their descriptions of early childhood may be based on information from parent, siblings, etc. since memory systems are not fully developed early in life. In addition, when describing future life stages they may have to consider familiar adults (e.g., parents, grandparents, professors) and try to anticipate what will be important when they reach these ages.

3. Stop the class after about 15 minutes. Go through the stages in order and ask students to give examples of what they wrote. Typically, they give the following examples:

   - **First Year**—Major concerns include being fed and nurtured, having diapers changed, etc. They may give examples of physical changes, beginning to speak, and cognitive changes such as recognizing faces. These provide good examples to use when discussing Erikson's notion of trust vs. mistrust.

   - **Second Year**—Major concerns include learning how to walk, potty training, feeding self, etc. They may talk about having temper tantrums, climbing onto counters, etc. Their examples are useful when discussing Erikson's autonomy vs. shame and doubt stage.

   - **Preschool Years**—Major concerns include playing, having friends, getting in trouble, learning how to ride a bike, discovering their own and other's sexuality. Discussion often includes memories of playing make believe. The students enjoy talking about who they pretended to be (e.g., He-Man, Ninja Turtles, and other super heroes). You may want to include an example of your own experience (e.g., getting in trouble for chopping down a newly planted tree because you needed lumber). By focusing on their creativity and imagination in this stage, a discussion of Erikson's initiative vs. guilt can follow.

   - **Grade School Years**—Major concerns include starting and doing well in school, making friends, playing sports and games, etc. They also may bring up accomplishments—being on sports teams, taking first place at a science fair, chess tournament or other school event. They also talk about disappointments—being picked on by other kids or siblings, being a bad athlete, having to be in special ed. classes, etc. These can be used to illustrate Erikson's industry vs. inferiority stage.

   - **Adolescence**—Major concerns include appearance, dating, and friends. For later adolescence they may bring up deciding to go to college or having a job. Students also relate to identifying with certain groups (e.g., high school cliques, clubs, teams, etc.). This discussion can be used to illustrate Erikson's identity vs. role confusion stage.

   - **Early Adulthood**—Major concerns include dating and finding a partner, relationships with friends, deciding on a career, doing well in college. Major accomplishments may include getting married, graduating from college, or landing a good job. The examples of relationship concerns can be used to discuss Erikson's intimacy vs. isolation stage.

- **Middle Adulthood**—Major concerns include children, careers, and making-money. Sometimes middle aged students volunteer to share what is important to them. This often includes supporting and raising children, changing careers, being a active member of the community, etc. This can be used to illustrate Erikson's generativity vs. stagnation.

- **Late Adulthood**—Major concerns include health, retirement, and losing loved ones and friends. Discussion can include what students think needs to happen for them to have a positive experience with this final stage. A discussion of Erikson's integrity vs. despair can follow.

4. If time permits, students may be asked if there are any sex differences associated with any of the stages. Ask them, by a show of hands, which stage of life is the best time of life. Many students will pick young adulthood, a few will pick late adulthood. Discuss stereotypes associated with aging.

# Your Life Span

1. First year of life (0–1)

2. Second year of life (1–2)

3. Preschool years (2–5)

4. Grade school years (5–12)

5. Adolescence (puberty–19)

6. Young Adulthood (20s)

7. Middle Adulthood (30s–50s)

8. Late Adulthood (60s and beyond)

# Assimilation and Accommodation

**(Adapted from Harper, 1979)**

The following activity will help students understand some basic Piagetian terms and relate better to the cognitive challenges faced by infants and young children.

**DEMONSTRATION:** The newborn is capable only of assimilating novel stimulation to existing reflexes such as rooting or sucking. In this demonstration students are invited to relive the exciting prospect of learning about (trying to make sense of, or equilibrate) a novel object, much as an infant does.

**MATERIALS:**
- A box big enough for the class to see (preferably black)
- (A shoe box covered in black paper will work)

**TIME:** Approximately 10 minutes

**PROCEDURES:**

1. Begin by presenting an imaginary object, called a gloquex (pronounced "glocks"), to the class. The gloquex does not really exist; pretend to remove it from a large, black box and place it on a table in front of the class. Do not tell them what the object is called.

2. Tell the class that the gloquex is a device weighing about 5 lbs. and measuring about 8 inches × 12 inches × 4 inches.

3. Plug the gloquex in and allow it to warm up.

4. Since you haven't mentioned the object's name, students will often spontaneously begin asking questions. The following are some hypothetical answers:
   a. What's it called? Gloquex.
   b. What does it do? It constructs negative electromagnetic waves or bad vibes in the classroom.
   c. How does it work? An inversely reciprocating frimfram bollixes any waves entering the aperture.
   d. What is it made of? Hyperventilated case-hardened mollox.
   e. Why can't I see it? You can't? (Followed by an incredulous look.)

5. After the question period, test students on their knowledge of gloques. Focus on its elements and how it works. The students' responses will be much like those of a child learning a new concept. They'll know its name and its primary purpose. Beyond that, however, they'll find it difficult to talk about. Because it fits no existing schema, they are likely to describe it by relying on phrases such as: "It's like a . . ." or "It's similar to a . . .," or "It's sort of like something I once saw on "Star Trek."

6. Point out that these answers reflect attempts to fit a novel stimulus into a previously existing experience (assimilation) or to modify schemas (accommodation). Learning about a gloquex is not unlike a very young child learning about a dog, a cat, or any unfamiliar object.

**Related Reading:**

Harper, G. F. (1979). Introducing Piagetian concepts through the use of familiar and novel illustrations. *Teaching of Psychology*, **6** (1), 58–59.

## Adolescent Sexuality

**(Adapted from Cauffman, 1999)**

**DEMONSTRATION:** This activity is a good prelude to a discussion of sexuality.

**MATERIALS:** None

**TIME:** Approximately three minutes

**PROCEDURES:**

1. Have students find a partner and have them raise their clasped hands so you can see that each one has a partner.

2. Next, have the class repeat after you the words "penis" and "vagina" twice.

3. Then ask the person on the right to turn to the person on the left and say "penis" while the person on the left says "vagina" at the same time.

4. This very brief "lecture launcher" gets the attention of the class, elicits a lot of giggling, and nicely illustrates the awkwardness most Americans have with sex as a topic of discussion. Follow the activity with a discussion about how different

societies socialize their younger members about sex (e.g., restrictive vs. semi-restrictive vs. permissive socialization beliefs).

5. We usually point out to students that their laughter is indicative of how uncomfortable they are and yet, the terms "penis" and "vagina" are probably not the more common terms they use for these anatomical body parts (imagine the discomfort more common pejorative terms would elicit!).

6. We then make the point that the United States is typically semi-restrictive about sexuality (e.g., if a teacher sees students in high school making-out in the hall he/she would intervene and tell them their behavior is inappropriate, yet, if the same person observed the same behavior at a mall, he/she would look the other way most likely). We then discuss the mixed messages this response communicates to teens and the high rate of problem behaviors related to sexuality our country evidences compared to other more permissive societies.

This "ice-breaker" activity loosens the atmosphere in the class such that students are more comfortable with the explicitness of a human sexuality lecture.

**Related Reading:**

Cauffman, E. (1999). **Instructor's Resource Manual with test questions to accompany Adolescence** (5th Edition). Boston: McGraw-Hill, Inc.

# Chapter 15

# Adult Development and Aging

---

## Who am I? (Identity)

### (Adapted from Bugen, 1979)

---

**DEMONSTRATION:** This activity introduces the concept of identity to adult students who are probably trying out different roles in their efforts to achieve a clear sense of who they are.

**MATERIALS:**
- One piece of notebook paper per student

**TIME:** Approximately 10 minutes

**PROCEDURES:**

1. Have students write down ten different answers to the question, "Who am I?" Give them a minute or so to get started on their own and then suggest that they may respond in terms of their social roles (e.g., dating partner) or responsibilities (e.g., student or worker or both), the groups they belong to, their beliefs, their personality traits or qualities, their needs, feelings, or behavior patterns. Instruct them to list only those that are really important to them, those that, if lost, would make a real difference in their sense of identity.

2. When they have completed their list, have them consider each item separately. Ask them to imagine what life would be like if that were no longer true. For example, what would the loss of a parent mean to those who wrote down "son" or "daughter"?

3. After students have reviewed items as instructed in #2, have them rank-order the items in terms of importance. To determine the rank of each item, they should consider the adjustment required if they "lost" the item.

4. Finally, lead a brief class discussion in which you ask students to share with the class what they discovered about their identity development. Encourage openness and comparison with others, although avoid forcing anyone to reveal anything

uncomfortable. Students may be surprised to find out how much they have in common with their peers in their search for an identity.

5. Results may be related to theories on identity (Erikson and Marcia) as covered in the text or in lectures.

**Related Readings:**

Bugen, L. A. (1979). **Death and dying.** Dubuque, Iowa: Wm. C. Brown.

Cauffman, E. (1999). **Instructor's Resource Manual with test questions to accompany Adolescence** (5th Edition). Boston: McGraw- Hill, Inc.

---

## Attraction & Choosing a Mate

---

The following activity may be used to involve students in a discussion of Erikson's intimacy vs. isolation stage. Since the majority of students in introductory classes are just beginning this stage (young adulthood), forming relationships seems to be of great interest to many of them. In later discussions, it may be used to illustrate gender or age differences. Finally, the activity may be used to introduce the topic of attraction if it is covered in the social psychology unit.

**DEMONSTRATION:** Students write a personal ad that includes important characteristics that they would look for in a mate.

**MATERIALS:**
- One piece of notebook paper per student

**TIME:** Approximately 10–15 minutes

**PROCEDURES:**

1. After introducing Erikson's notion of intimacy vs. isolation, tell students that you want to take a few minutes to explore their concept of an ideal mate. Ask them to take out a piece of notebook paper and construct a personal ad that includes the characteristics they desire in an ideal mate.

2. To begin discussion, ask students to volunteer various characteristics that are important to them. Jot these characteristics down on the overhead projector. Usually

the first characteristics that are mentioned describe personality-type qualities (e.g., honest, good sense of humor, achievement-oriented, athletic) and similar values and interests (e.g., like to dance or go to movies, gets involved in political issues, likes rap music, etc.). Someone will eventually call out—physical attractiveness. The class usually finds this humorous and laughs.

3. Use the list of examples to demonstrate how "potential" mates seem to be put through a series of hurdles. The first hurdle involves proximity. This rarely is an example given by the class. However, when the class is asked to think of a close friendship formed since coming to campus—they will typically find that person lived nearby them or sat by them in a class. It's fun to mention that they should look around at those sitting next to them—just in case there is a potential mate. The second hurdle involves physical appearance. Here talk about what is considered physically attractive and the matching hypothesis. The third hurdle includes dispositional factors (personality, values, attitudes, etc.). Ask if opposites or similar others seem to be most attractive. The fourth hurdle includes similar interests. Discuss why similar interests are important. Finally, the fifth hurdle is readiness. At this point, discuss that an individual could have made it over all the previous hurdles, however, he or she may still not be an ideal mate. At this point, discuss readiness and how fixation in an early stage (e.g., trust vs. mistrust) may block intimacy.

4. During the above discussions, references to gender or age differences may be made. For example, is physical attractiveness more important to men than women? Do older students look for different dispositional characteristics than younger students? Why do these differences occur?

---

## How Much Do You Know About Aging?

**(Adapted from Atwater & Duffy, 1998)**

---

The following activity tests students' knowledge of aging by presenting a short test developed by Atwater and Duffy (1998). It helps students confront their own erroneous beliefs about old age.

**DEMONSTRATION:** Students take a short test on aging. Answers are presented and discussed.

**MATERIALS:**
- One piece of notebook paper per student

**TIME:** Approximately 10 minutes

**PROCEDURE:**

1. Before discussing older adulthood, students take a short quiz on aging. Ask students to use a piece of notebook paper to respond to the following 10 true-false questions—which you will read out loud from an overhead transparency (see **OHT 15.1**).

    1. All five senses tend to decline in old age.
    2. People lose about one-third of their brain cells or neurons by late adulthood.
    3. Drivers over 65 years of age have fewer traffic accidents per person than those under 30.
    4. Older people are more alike than younger people.
    5. People become less susceptible to short-term illnesses, such as the common cold, as they age.
    6. Recognition memory declines sharply with old age.
    7. Reaction time generally becomes slower with age.
    8. About one-fourth of those over 65 live in nursing homes.
    9. People become more fearful of death as they grow older.
    10. Widows outnumber widowers about three to one.

2. After presenting students the ten questions, read the correct answers so that they can score their own tests. The answers are as follows:

    1. **TRUE.** Aspects of hearing, vision, and touch decline in old age. For many people, taste and smell become less sensitive.
    2. **FALSE.** People lose very few neurons (only about 7%). The loss begins in middle adulthood (around age 30), not in old age.
    3. **TRUE.** Older adults have fewer accidents than people under age 30. However, they have more accidents than middle-aged adults.
    4. **FALSE.** There is as much variety between older people as there is between younger people (maybe more).
    5. **TRUE.** Older people are less susceptible to short-term aliments such as the common cold. This is attributed to an accumulation of antigens. However, older adults are more susceptible to life-threatening ailments.
    6. **FALSE.** Recognition memory shows little or no decline with age. However, there is a decline in recall memory.
    7. **TRUE.** Reaction time declines with age.
    8. **FALSE.** Only about 5% of people over 65 live in nursing homes.
    9. **FALSE.** Older people may think more about death, but they tend to have less fear than other age groups.
    10. **TRUE.** Widows outnumber widowers about 3 to 1.

3. Ask the class to indicate by a show of hands how many scored a perfect ten on the test. Very few will raise their hands. Use the data as evidence that the class has a lot to learn about growing older.

**Related Reading:**

Atwater, E. and Duffy, K. G. (1999). **Psychology for Living** (6th Edition). Englewood Cliffs, NJ: Prentice-Hall.

# TRUE or FALSE

1. All five senses tend to decline in old age.

2. People lose about one-third of their brain cells or neurons by late adulthood.

3. Drivers over 65 years of age have fewer traffic accidents per person than those under 30.

4. Older people are more alike than younger people.

5. People become less susceptible to short-term illnesses, such as the common cold, as they age.

6. Recognition memory declines sharply with old age.

7. Reaction time generally becomes slower with age.

8. About one-fourth of those over 65 live in nursing homes.

9. People become more fearful of death as they grow older.

10. Widows outnumber widowers about three to one.

# Chapter 16

# Personality

We have found that if students know nothing else about psychology, they know something about Sigmund Freud. Unfortunately, most of their associations around Freud and Freudian thought are quite negative—weird, fixated on sex, cocaine addict, etc. We find the following brief activity a useful way of encouraging students to reconsider Freud's contributions to psychology. After going through this activity, we find students give Freud a little more respect. Additionally, students are exposed to some of the key components of Freud's theory (the role of the unconscious, the importance of early childhood experiences on later development, etc.) in a way that helps them remember the concepts.

**DEMONSTRATION:** Students respond to a brief true/false quiz on core Freudian principles.

**MATERIALS:**
- One page of notebook paper per student

**TIME:** Approximately 10 minutes

**PROCEDURES:**

1. Before beginning your discussion of the psychoanalytic approach to understanding personality, ask students to take out a sheet of notebook paper. Have them number their sheet from 1 to 5.

2. Ask students to listen to the following five statements (see **OHT 16.1**) and indicate whether they believe the statement to be True of them or False. Depending on the points an instructor makes in lecture, he/she may want to add statements or substitute statements to the list given below.

   a. I believe my parents have been one of the most influential forces in my development.
   b. Events that occurred in childhood still affect me today.

     c.  I sometimes experience a struggle from within myself—such as when tempted to eat a high-calorie dessert.

     d.  Sometimes I am not aware of my own motivations and desires.

     e.  Sometimes when I am in an argument with someone, I feel they assume that I am upset, when I am actually fine.

3. After students have responded, ask for a show of hands to see what proportion of the class agreed or disagreed with each of the statements. It has been our experience that approximately two-thirds of the class usually endorse all of the statements.

4. Ask students if they know what common feature is shared by all of the statements. Usually someone who is ahead in their reading is able to figure it out. What the statements have in common is that they are consistent with the major principles underlying Freud's theory of personality development.

5. Ask students if they would have predicted that they would have agreed with Freud's ideas before this activity. Many students are genuinely surprised that Freud is not the weirdo that they have always believed him to be. Lead the class in a discussion of Freud's legacy to psychology. Point out that many of Freud's ideas are still embraced by contemporary psychologists . . . the concept of the unconscious, the import of early childhood experiences, the use of defense mechanisms to maintain a positive self-concept, etc.

6. Optional: We will often use this as in-class extra credit/attendance check by collecting students' papers.

**OHT 16.1**

---

**TRUE or FALSE**

A. I believe my parents have been one of the most influential forces in my development.

B. Events that occurred in childhood still affect me today.

C. I sometimes experience a struggle from within myself—such as when tempted to eat a high-calorie dessert.

D. Sometimes I am not aware of my own motivations and desires.

E. Sometimes when I am in an argument with someone, I feel they assume that I am upset, when I am actually fine.

---

# Carl Rogers' Person-Centered Approach

Students usually enjoy the area of personality because they can relate the material to themselves and others. The following activity gives students an opportunity to gain some insight on their concept of self. In addition, it can be used to illustrate several important components in Rogers' theory of personality. These include: the role of the self-concept, unconditional positive regard, self-actualization, and maladjustment.

**DEMONSTRATION:** Students write a description of their perceived and ideal selves.

**MATERIALS:**
- Two pages of notebook paper per student Transparencies or PowerPoint slides

**TIME:** Approximately 30 minutes

**PROCEDURES:**

1. After a brief introduction to the Humanistic approach to personality, ask students to take out two sheets of notebook paper. Have them label one sheet "Perceived Self" and the other sheet "Ideal Self." Ask them to spend about 10 minutes writing down a description of how they perceive themselves. It is helpful to give them some examples of what you would write about yourself (you can usually describe something about yourself that they find humorous).

2. Stop them after 10 minutes and ask them to take out the sheet labeled "Ideal Self." Begin this part of the demonstration by saying you are going to indulge them in some fantasy time—now they can describe who they would like to be. Again, ask the class to spend about 10 minutes on this description.

3. Again stop the class after 10 minutes. Ask the class if anyone wrote exactly the same thing on both pages. The likely response is that no one will have described the perceived and ideal selves in the same way. Then make the statement that a fully-functioning, self-actualized individual would have raised his or her hand because the perceived self is completely congruent with the ideal self.

4. If time allows, the class usually enjoys brainstorming reasons why this complete overlap doesn't occur for most of us (e.g., they are still maturing or growing; there are parts of themselves that they don't like and would like to become better people; there are things about themselves that other people don't like, etc.).

5. At this point, describe that our beliefs and feelings about ourselves are central to Carl Rogers' theory of personality. Our major motivation (or the core of personality) is self-actualization. Self-actualization is the process of completely knowing and accepting ourselves. So, according to Rogers our major motivation is to achieve congruence between who we think we are (the description on Paper 1), who we really are (the actual person sitting in the chair), and who we want to be (the description on Paper 2).

6. Use the overhead transparency 16.2 included with this demonstration (or, transfer it to a power point demonstration) to reinforce the above concept. In addition, you can add to this transparency while lecturing. This will help in demonstrating how parts of the Real Self may be "deleted" from our self-concept (e.g., we may deny that we experience anger), or that parts of the Ideal Self are characteristics that we think our parents want us to have that we do not have (e.g., being athletic).

7. Lead a lecture on how the self-concept develops—through conditional and unconditional positive regard. Tie the overlapping selves to UCPR and CPR to the incongruent selves.

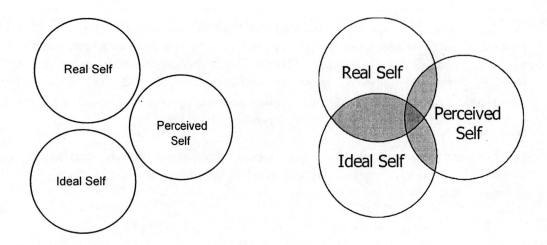

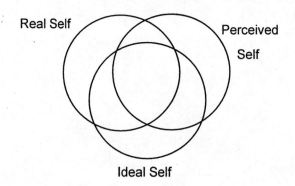

## A Covert Test of Public Self-Consciousness

**(Adapted from Bolt, 1999)**

The following brief activity illustrates a personality characteristic that most students can relate to: self-consciousness. The instructor engages in the following activity described below with students and then discusses the concept of public vs. private self-consciousness. We find this a useful technique to begin the discussion of personality characteristics. Instructors also can use this activity to discuss non-self-report measures of personality.

**DEMONSTRATION:** Students draw a capital "E" on a piece of paper on their forehead. Depending on the orientation of the letter, students are either inferred to be either high in public or private self-consciousness.

**MATERIALS**:
■   One page of notebook paper per student

**TIME**: Approximately 10 minutes

**PROCEDURES**:

1.  This activity works well either as an introduction to personality issues or as a demonstration of more "covert" means of measuring personality.

2.  Ask students to take out a sheet of paper and place it on their foreheads.

3.  Have students draw a capital "E" on the sheet of paper using their dominant hand.

4.  Then ask students what direction does the "E" face?

5.  According to research by Hass (1984), if the "E" is oriented so that someone looking at the student would see it in the correct position, it is likely that the student is high in public self-consciousness. Those who are high in public self-consciousness tend to be more concerned with physical appearance and how others perceive them. Such individuals also are more likely to be sensitive to what others think of them, and may be more likely to conform to other's beliefs as a way of avoiding negative evaluations.

6. If students draw the "E" so that the they themselves could read it, Hass suggests that it is likely that they are low in public self-consciousness (having drawn the letter from an internal perspective).

7. Lead the class in a discussion of public vs. private self-consciousness. Explain that those high in private self-consciousness are more likely to focus on individual factors such as moods, emotions, sensations. A sample self-report item for the private self-consciousness subscale is, "I reflect about myself a lot." Those high in public self-consciousness, on the other hand, tend to focus on how they are perceived by others. A sample item from the public self-consciousness subscale is, "One of the last things I do before I leave my house is look in the mirror."

8. We find that students are often skeptical about how much this mini-demonstration really tells about levels of self-consciousness in particular and personality in general. We like to channel this skepticism into a discussion of the various ways we use to measure personality (e.g., self-report, covert behavioral, physiological techniques). We discuss triangulation of research methods and explain to students how convergent evidence from multiple techniques of measuring personality gives the researcher/clinician more confidence in their judgments of another's personality.

**Related Readings:**

Bolt, M. (1999). Public and private self-consciousness. In **Instructor's Manual to accompany D. Myers' Social Psychology** (6th Edition). New York: McGraw-Hill Inc.

Hass, R. (1984). Perspective taking and self-awareness. *Journal of Personality and Social Psychology*, **46**, 788–798.

# Chapter 17

# Stress and Health

## How Hardy Are You?

**(Adapted from Kobasa, 1979)**

Susan Kobasa and her colleagues examined the relationship between stress and health in 200 telephone executives at risk for illness due to the nature of their jobs (although they were in good health at the time of the study). They examined three personality traits: commitment to self, work, family, and other important values; a sense of personal control over one's life; and the ability to see change in one's life as a challenge to master. They found that the healthiest executives were not younger, wealthier, higher on the career ladder, or better educated than their colleagues who became sick under stress. Rather, they were "hardier."

**DEMONSTRATION:** This activity allows students to examine Kobasa's three "C's" (commitment, control, and challenge) in themselves and obtain an overall assessment of their "psychological hardiness." According to Kobasa, hardier people should be better able to face change with confidence and self-determination, and see change as opportunity compared to less hardy people.

**MATERIALS:**
- One piece of notebook paper per student

**TIME:** Approximately 10–15 minutes

**PROCEDURES:**

1. Before lecturing on stress and health, ask students to complete the short survey on the next page (this may be presented as an overhead transparency, see **OHT 17.1**).

2. After students have completed the survey, indicate that the questions measure control, commitment, and challenge. Tell them that for half of the questions, a high score (like 3, "strongly agree") indicates hardiness; while for the other half of the questions a low score (disagreement) does not.

3. Next, go over the following scoring instructions carefully with the students: To get scores on control, commitment, and challenge, first write the number of your answer (0, 1, 2, or 3) above the letter of each question on the scoring grid below the questions. Then add and subtract as indicated. (To get your score on "control," for example, add your answers to questions A and G; add your answers to B and H; and then subtract the second number from the first.) Add scores on commitment, control, and challenge for a total hardiness score. (See **OHT 17.2**.)

A total score of 10–18 shows a hardy personality; 0–9 indicates moderate hardiness; and below 0 is low hardiness.

**Related Reading:**

Kobasa, S. C. (1979). Stressful life events, personality, and health: An inquiry into hardiness. *Journal of Personality and Social Psychology*, **37**, 1–11.

# How Hardy Are You?

Below are 12 items similar to those appearing on a measure of "hardiness." Evaluating someone's hardiness requires more than this brief survey; yet this simple exercise should give you some idea of how hardy you are.

Write down how much you agree or disagree with the following statements, using this scale:

**0 = strongly disagree**      **2 = mildly agree**
**1 = mildly disagree**      **3 = strongly agree**

____ A.     Trying my best at work (or school) makes a difference.

____ B.     Trusting to fate is sometimes all I can do in a relationship.

____ C.     I often wake up eager to start on the day's projects.

____ D.     Thinking of myself as a free person leads to great frustration and difficulty.

____ E.     I would be willing to sacrifice financial security in my work if something really challenging came along.

____ F.     It bothers me when I have to deviate from the routine or schedule I've set for myself.

____ G.     An average citizen can have an impact on politics.

____ H.     Without the right breaks, it is hard to be successful in my field.

____ I.     I know why I am doing what I am doing at work (or school).

____ J.     Getting close to people puts me at risk of being obligated to them.

____ K.     Encountering new situations is an important priority in my life.

____ L.     I really don't mind when I have nothing to do.

# Scoring Grid for Hardiness Scale

$$\overline{A} + \overline{G} = \underline{\quad}$$

$$-$$

$$\overline{B} + \overline{H} = \underline{\quad} = \underline{\qquad}$$
Control
Score

$$\overline{C} + \overline{I} = \underline{\quad}$$

$$-$$

$$\overline{D} + \overline{J} = \underline{\quad} = \underline{\qquad}$$
Commitment
Score

$$\overline{E} + \overline{K} = \underline{\quad}$$

$$-$$

$$\overline{F} + \overline{L} = \underline{\quad} = \underline{\qquad}$$
Challenge
Score

$$\overline{\quad\quad} + \overline{\quad\quad} + \overline{\quad\quad} = \overline{\quad\quad}$$
Control + Commitment + Challenge = Total Hardiness
Score

Total Score of: 10–18 = Hardy Personality; 0–9 = Moderately Hardy Personality; Below 0 = Low Hardiness

## Type A Personality and the Stress Response

The following activity can be used to help students recognize Type A tendencies in themselves. This brief activity personalizes the accompanying lecture material.

**DEMONSTRATION:** Students estimate the passage of time.

**MATERIALS:**
- Stop watch or clock

**TIME:** Approximately 5 minutes

**PROCEDURES:**

1. Before introducing this exercise, it is helpful to familiarize students with the concept of stress (what it is, why we experience it, what are negative and positive outcomes associated with stress). Then introduce the idea that different people seem to respond to similar situations in different ways.

2. Tell the class that you will be giving them a brief "test", but this one is an easy test—you just want them to put their heads down on their desks and close their eyes. All they have to do is respond by raising their hands when they believe a minute has elapsed.

3. Ask the class if they are ready, then tell them to start. You will notice that some students raise their hands before 30 seconds have elapsed, other students have yet to raise their hands after 60 seconds.

4. Stop the class after 60 seconds. Many students are surprised by how long it takes for a minute to elapse. Have students who underestimated the time raise their hands. Then ask these students a series of questions relating to the Type A behavioral pattern—Do they find themselves hurrying to get places when they have plenty of time? Do they avoid situations where they have to wait? Do they like competition? Do they engage in more than one activity at a time? Do they feel angry when they are interrupted?, etc.

5. Lead a lecture on the various components of the Type A behavioral pattern and how it relates to experiencing stress.

# The Powerful Need for Control

**(Adapted from Dollinger, 1990)**

The following activity based on Dollinger (1990) illustrates our powerful need to feel that we can control events (even events that are beyond our control). For example, Dollinger notes that one's odds of winning the lottery do not change as a function of choosing or being assigned a ticket and yet people feel more confident when they can actively choose their own numbers rather than passively being supplied with the numbers. This activity can be used in a variety of different ways. For example, it can be used to get across how important the perception of control is for individuals in terms of stress and health issues (feeling a sense of control over one's body, making decisions regarding one's own treatment, having a say in work-related issues, etc.). The activity also can be used to help students understand compulsive gambling and superstitious behavior. In this activity, students either choose or are assigned a playing card by the instructor. The student with the highest card wins $1.00. Students estimate their probability of winning the dollar. Those students who felt as if they had control over the event (had the opportunity to choose their own card) report that they have more confidence that they will win the money. Thus, even in purely chance situations (Langer, 1975), we may feel more confident of the outcome if we can exert any measure of control. Students enjoy this activity and an additional benefit is that it can involve a large number of students.

**DEMONSTRATION:** Students either choose or are assigned a playing card. The student with the highest card will win $1.00. Each student writes down what they believe to be their probability of winning the dollar. Additional members of the class calculate the mean probability rating per group (assigned or choice of card group).

**MATERIALS**:
- Approximately 22 students (10 persons per group + an additional 2 students to calculate the mean ratings in each group)
- One deck of playing cards
- One page of notebook paper per student
- A $1.00 bill
- Two blank overhead transparency pages

**TIME**: Approximately 20–25 minutes

**PROCEDURES**:

1. As you begin the lecture, take out a dollar bill and announce to the class that they will be taking part in a brief card game. State that the person with the highest card will win the dollar. (Note: You may want to establish what card suit "rules" in the event that some students choose the same card from different suits).

2. Ask for twenty-two volunteers. Line up 20 of them in the front of the class. Hand a card to the first person, direct the second to choose his or her card, and alternate in this fashion until all twenty students have a card. TELL STUDENTS NOT TO LOOK AT THEIR CARDS. TELL THE REST OF THE CLASS TO MAKE SURE THAT THEY DON'T CHEAT!!

3. After students each have a card, ask students BEFORE they have looked at their card, to write down what level of confidence they have that they hold the highest card from 0–100%.

4. After students have made their ratings, have them turn over their cards and determine who has the highest card. Award the dollar.

5. Now have the remaining 2 volunteers each calculate the composite mean rating of the two groups (choice or no choice). Ask the 2 volunteers to write down the ten percentages and the mean percentage on an overhead transparency.

6. Consistent with the illusion of control, students who had the opportunity to choose their own card should be more confident that they hold the winning card than students who had no control over the situation. Show students the overheads.

7. Dollinger (1998) reported that students in the choice condition report markedly higher mean percentages ($M = 55\%$) than those in the no-choice group ($M = 45\%$). He also notes that both groups tend to be overconfident given the number of those participating in the activity.

8. Lead the class in a discussion of why this effect occurs. Why is it important for us to believe that we have control over situations (even those when we actually do not!)? What are the advantages and disadvantages to possessing this bias. For example, is holding such a bias beneficial or detrimental to one's mental health? Can students think of other situations in which it is important for us to believe that we exercise control (e.g., the progression of illness; work-related outcomes, ESP tasks, etc.). How does this illusion play out in terms of superstitions? Do students engage in any kind of superstitious activities before an important exam, a big game, etc.? Does the behavior actually impact the outcome or does the belief and corresponding behavior work to reduce feelings of anxiety?

**Related Readings:**

Dollinger, S. J. (1998). The illusion of control. In **Activities handbook for the teaching of psychology** (Vol. **3**). Washington, DC: American Psychological Association.

Langer, E. J. (1975). The illusion of control. *Journal of Personality and Social Psychology*, **32**, 311–328.

# Chapter 18

## Abnormal Behavior

Misconceptions About
Mental Disorders

(Adapted from Cleary, 1996)

**DEMONSTRATION:** This activity demonstrates that most of us have some misconceptions about mental illness. Students take a brief True or False quiz on mental illness.

**MATERIALS:**
- One sheet of notebook paper per student

**TIME:** Approximately 5 minutes

**PROCEDURES:**

1. Before lecturing on abnormal behavior, ask students to take out a piece of paper to use for a short quiz on mental illness. Ask students to record either True or False for each of the statements you will be reading out loud.

2. Ask students to respond to the following seven questions as True or False. (If you wish, make an overhead transparency from the list of questions included at the end of this activity, see **OHT 18.1**.)

   A. Abnormal behaviors are always bizarre.
   B. A clear distinction can be drawn between "normal" and "abnormal" behaviors.
   C. As a group, former mental patients are unpredictable and dangerous.
   D. Mental disorders indicate a fundamental deficiency in personality and are thus shameful.
   E. Since mental illness is so common, there is reason to be fearful of one's own vulnerability.
   F. Geniuses are particularly prone to emotional disorders.
   G. Most mental disorders are incurable.

3. Have students correct their responses. All of the answers are false.

4. Follow up with a discussion about why each of the questions are false. Below are some details about each of the questions.

   A. Abnormal behaviors are always bizarre. The media may perpetuate this view because extreme behaviors are reported. In addition, movies and novels may play up extreme behavior because it is intriguing and captures attention.

   B. A clear distinction can be drawn between "normal" and "abnormal" behaviors. Abnormality is a matter of degree. There are not two distinct categories (normal vs. abnormal). Abnormality represents a poor fit between behavior and the situation.

   C. As a group, former mental patients are unpredictable and dangerous. The average former mental patient is no more unpredictable or dangerous than people in general. Again, the media may promote this image.

   D. Mental disorders indicate a fundamental deficiency in personality, and are thus shameful. Everyone shares the potential for behaving abnormally. In addition, why should mental disorders be more "shameful" than physical disorders?

   E. Since mental illness is so common, there is reason to be fearful of one's own vulnerability. The average person is not likely to have a mental disorder. If this does occur, the individual has an excellent chance of fully recovering.

   F. Geniuses are particularly prone to emotional disorders. According to Terman's research on high IQ children, the opposite may be true. Higher IQ people may be better adjusted than the general population.

   G. Most mental disorders are incurable. Between 70–80% of people hospitalized for mental disorders recover.

**Related Reading:**

Cleary R. J. (1996). Misconceptions about mental disorders. In **Instructor's Resource Manual to accompany Wade & Tavris Psychology** (4th Edition), Glenview: Addison Wesley Longman.

# TRUE or FALSE

A. Abnormal behaviors are always bizarre.

B. A clear distinction can be drawn between "normal" and "abnormal" behaviors.

C. As a group, former mental patients are unpredictable and dangerous.

D. Mental disorders indicate a fundamental deficiency in personality and are thus shameful.

E. Since mental illness is so common, there is reason to be fearful of one's own vulnerability.

F. Geniuses are particularly prone to emotional disorders.

G. Most mental disorders are incurable.

# What's Normal?

This activity exposes students to the difficulty in distinguishing abnormal from normal behavior. Students are given an opportunity to consider various criteria used to identify and define abnormal behavior. They will see that not everyone, including psychologists, agrees on what is normal.

**DEMONSTRATION:** For large classes, having students discuss the material with a person sitting next to them works well. Allow students to view an overhead containing four or five brief vignettes each describing an individual's behavior (see next page). Ask them to determine if the behavior is normal or abnormal and provide a rationale for their judgments. A class discussion of criteria used for defining abnormal behavior should follow the activity.

**MATERIALS:**
- One page handout (see **Handout 18.1**)

**TIME:** Approximately 20 minutes

**PROCEDURES:**

1. Introduce this activity by giving students an obvious example of abnormal behavior (for example, a case of multiple personality disorder). Then, tell students that unfortunately determinations of abnormality are not always so easy to recognize.

2. Ask students to pair up with a person sitting next to them. Have the pairs discuss whether or not the four vignettes are examples of abnormal behavior. Have them discuss rationales for their opinions.

3. Once they have had an opportunity to talk about each vignette, the whole class may discuss the criteria for defining abnormality. These may include: norm violations, statistical deviations, personal discomfort (self and other), impairment of functioning, and deviations from an ideal. The role of biology versus environmental causes of disorders can be explored. In addition, the discussion lends itself to a consideration of the dangers and limitations of labeling.

## What's Normal?

1. Allison Ames is a twenty-year old college senior. She is independent and determined to live life her own way. She and her boyfriend of one year enjoy sexual relations often. She likes to spend her time studying, listening to music, and socializing with friends. She and her boyfriend, along with friends, smoke pot about twice a week. Allison wants others to enjoy life as much as she does. She is active in trying to persuade the state legislature to pass new laws regarding marijuana use and private adult sexual behavior. **Is Allison's behavior normal or abnormal? Why?**

2. Betty Burns is a forty-year-old homemaker whose two children are grown and living on their own. Betty's husband is an active business man who frequently travels. In addition he is an avid sports fan and enjoys spending his spare time at sporting events with his male friends. Betty has few interests outside her home and spends considerable time by herself. She would like to spend more time with her husband, but he resists. Betty is very lonely. Recently she has increased her cigarette consumption and begun to drink three cocktails before eating dinner, and two more before going to bed. **Is Betty's behavior normal or abnormal? Why?**

3. Caleb Cunningham is a six-year-old boy who come from a family situation characterized by physical abuse. In school he is aggressive and mean to other children. Caleb's teachers have tried to work with him, however, his behavior continues. This week Caleb was sent to the principal, who took away Caleb's recess privileges for three days. **Is Caleb's behavior normal or abnormal? Why?**

4. David and Debbie Duncan have been married for ten years. They have a two-year-old daughter. They are miserable and have sought out a marriage counselor. They frequently disagree and fight about budget issues, child rearing practices, and leisure activities. Whenever they fight, David becomes verbally aggressive and then storms out of the room. He stays distant for several days. Debbie starts to cry as soon as David raises his voice. She claims that he is making her depressed and hurting her badly. She wants to leave the relationship. They have decided to try counseling for the child's sake. **Is David's behavior normal or abnormal? Why? Is Debbie's behavior normal or abnormal? Why?**

## Learned Helplessness

**(Adapted from Cauffman, 1999)**

**DEMONSTRATION:** Learned helplessness is the belief that one cannot control forces in one's environment. This is a demonstration that can be done in the classroom to give students the sense of learned helplessness.

**MATERIALS:**
- An accomplice who will make a great deal of noise outside the classroom a few minutes after class begins. (You might garner two students from the class previous to the one in which you want to use this activity and have them come to class a few minutes late and get into an argument just outside the classroom.)

**TIME:** Approximately 10 minutes

**PROCEDURES:**

1. Present students with a "pop" quiz that involves several extremely difficult bogus questions (essays will work best). You might instead have them try to solve a series of complex logic puzzles, telling them that their performance will give an indication of their IQ.

2. While students are taking the quiz, have an accomplice outside the classroom begin making a great deal of noise, or introduce some other noxious stimulant. Our lecture halls have ceiling fans and if it is warm in the class on the day we use this activity we turn the fans off (instead of on) and if it is cool, we turn them on (instead of off). We also sometimes make up a quiz in a small font that is very difficult to read off the overhead.

3. The students should soon begin to become frustrated. Appear to get the noise stopped (unsuccessfully, of course) and inform the class that the noise is unavoidable.

4. Several minutes later, admit your deception and tell the class that the quiz is bogus. You should also have the accomplice end the noise at this point for real.

5. Ask students how they felt during the quiz. Proceed with a discussion on learned helplessness pointing out that the frustrated feelings students experienced for just a few minutes at the beginning of class characterize the typical feelings of someone with learned helplessness.

**Related Reading:**

Cauffman, E. (1999). **Instructor's Resource Manual with test questions to accompany Adolescence** (5th Edition). Boston: McGraw-Hill, Inc.

---

## Are You Drinking Too Much Alcohol?

**(Adapted from Kunz & Finkel, 1987)**

---

Students may be surprised to find that alcohol abuse is a disorder included in the DSM-IV. However, it is common health hazard for many people. Atwater and Duffy (1999) estimate that at least 1 out of 10 adults is a heavy drinker. The portion is highest among young males between the ages of 18 and 25. The following activity may personalize alcohol abuse for students who see themselves or their friends reflected in the 10-item survey presented below. This survey was developed by Kunz and Finkel (1987).

**DEMONSTRATION:** Students respond to a 10-item survey on drinking alcohol. The implications of their answers are discussed.

**MATERIALS:**
- One sheet of notebook paper per student
- Overhead transparency (see OHT 18.2)

**TIME:** Approximately 10 minutes

**PROCEDURES:**

1. After introducing the topic of substance abuse, ask students to use a piece of notebook paper to respond to the following 10-item survey on the overhead projector (you will need to make an overhead of the questions as included at the end of this activity, see **OHT 18.2**). Read aloud each question. Students should indicate YES or NO for each question.

   1. Do you often drink alone, either at home or in a bar?
   2. When holding an empty glass at a party, do you actively look for a refill instead of waiting to be offered one?
   3. Do you feel you must have a drink at a particular time every day such as after work?

4. Is your drinking ever a direct result of a quarrel, or do quarrels seem to occur when you've had a drink or two?

5. Do you ever miss work (or school) or scheduled meetings because of your drinking?

6. When questioned, do you ever lie about how much you drink?

7. Do you feel physically deprived if you cannot have at least one drink every day?

8. When you are under a lot of stress, do you automatically take a drink to "settle your nerves?"

9. Do you sometimes crave a drink in the morning?

10. Do you sometimes have "mornings after" when you can't remember what happened the night before?

2. After presenting students the 10 items, have them count the number of time they answered YES. Tell them that every YES response should be taken as a warning sign. TWO YES responses suggest that the individual may be developing a dependency on alcohol. THREE or more YES responses indicate a serious drinking problem that might require professional help.

3. Some students may disagree that saying YES to these items signals alcohol abuse. They often use the argument that drinking is just a part of normal social activity in college. This can lead to a discussion of how alcohol abuse seems to be the result of an interaction between physiology and culture. Discussion of treatment for alcohol addiction can follow.

**Related Readings:**

Atwater, E. & Duffy, K. G. (1999). **Psychology for Living** (6th Edition). Englewood Cliffs, NJ: Prentice-Hall.

Kunz, J.R.M. & Finkel, A. J. (Eds.) (1987). **The American Medical Association Family Medical Guide** by the American Medical Association. New York: Random House.

# ARE YOU DRINKING TOO MUCH ALCOHOL?

1. Do you often drink alone, either at home or in a bar?

2. When holding an empty glass at a party, do you actively look for a refill instead of waiting to be offered one?

3. Do you feel you must have a drink at a particular time every day such as after work?

4. Is your drinking ever a direct result of a quarrel, or do quarrels seem to occur when you've had a drink or two?

5. Do you ever miss work (or school) or scheduled meetings because of your drinking?

6. When questioned, do you ever lie about how much you drink?

7. Do you feel physically deprived if you cannot have at least one drink every day?

8. When you are under a lot of stress, do you automatically take a drink to "settle your nerves?"

9. Do you sometimes crave a drink in the morning?

10. Do you sometimes have "mornings after" when you can't remember what happened the night before?

# Chapter 19

# Treatment of Abnormal Behavior

## Ethical Issues
## Pertaining to Therapy

**(Adapted from Ciccarelli, 1999)**

**DEMONSTRATION:** Ethical issues around psychological treatment of patients seem rather straightforward, but often the issues are not so obvious. This activity involves holding a class discussion around four central ethical issues relevant to psychological treatment.

**MATERIALS:** None

**TIME:** Approximately 20 minutes

**PROCEDURES:**

1.  Ask the class if they think there is ever a time when sex with an ex-client or former patient is not seen as unethical.

    The American Psychological Association (APA) struggles with this question rather incessantly (see **OHT 19.1**). The latest APA ethical guidelines state that:

    -   Therapists must wait a minimum of two years before engaging sexually with a former client;
    -   Therapists must take into account the patient's current mental status, and must demonstrate that there was no exploitation of the client;
    -   Termination of treatment for the client was not for the purpose of eventual sexual intimacies;
    -   There would be little or no adverse impact on the client, and
    -   Behavior during the course of therapy on the part of the therapist was not in the service of inviting a post-termination sexual or romantic relationship with the client.

    Conversely, it is thought that a therapist cannot be effective with a former sexual partner.

2. Ask the class if they think you could be someone's therapist and his/her professor.

Dual roles of this nature do not work. It is recognized by APA and practicing psychologists that ideally all dual roles of this nature should be avoided, yet the reality is that all practicing professionals, regardless of their profession, invariably find themselves confronted with a dual role. This problem increases as the size of the community decreases, with rural practicing professionals more keenly aware of the dilemma.

3. Ask the class if it is sensible to take credit cards for psychotherapy services rendered and why or why not.

If it is clear that the client has no issues around money management and is obviously a responsible individual financial matters and merely prefers to pay with a credit card for financial history reasons, then a therapist might allow the use of credit cards. Otherwise, credit card use is not recommended for a variety of reasons such as the fact that credit card debt may complicate therapy or the dual role the therapist may enter by becoming a credit extender in addition to a therapist for a client.

4. Ask the class if they think it is ever ethical to refuse treatment to someone.

The best answer to this is "yes". If a therapist feels that he or she is unable to perform effectively, then he or she is obligated to refer the client elsewhere. Reasons for ineffectiveness include lack of training in the presenting problem, lack of training in the cultural issues of the client, or if the therapist believes that values held by the client are in conflict with his or her own and this conflict would impede therapy, then a referral is warranted. For instance an African American therapist would likely find it difficult being effective with a client who was a member of the Aryan Nation, or a therapist who was gay or lesbian may find it difficult being effective with a client who was a Neo-Nazi.

**Related Reading:**

Ciccarelli, S. (1999). **Instructor's manual to accompany Feldman's Understanding Psychology** (5th Edition). Boston: McGraw-Hill, Inc.

# APA Ethical Guidelines state that:

– Therapists must wait a minimum of two years before engaging sexually with a former client;

– Therapists must take into account the patient's current mental status, and must demonstrate that there was no exploitation of the client;

– Termination of treatment for the client was not for the purpose of eventual sexual intimacies;

– There would be little or no adverse impact on the client, and

– Behavior during the course of therapy on the part of the therapist was not in the service of inviting a post-termination sexual or romantic relationship with the client.

## Exploring Rational-Emotive Therapy Through Irrational Beliefs

**(Adapted from Eison, 1987)**

The following brief activity allows students to explore Rational-Emotive Therapy (Ellis, 1962; 1993) by working with some of the irrational beliefs (iBs) they may hold regarding test-taking. Students pair up and describe some of the recurring thoughts they have when they are getting ready to take an exam or are in the middle of taking an exam. After laying out some of the common irrational thoughts that are generated during an exam, the class provides examples of more effective thought patterns that may enhance exam performance. This activity tends to be a winner for a variety of reasons. First, students are given an opportunity to briefly socialize (which tends not to happen in larger sections). Second, the activity encourages them to commiserate with one another about one of their favorite subjects . . . the dreaded exam experience. Third, through this experience students are given a first-hand chance to see that they are not the only ones who experience such thoughts; a certain level of universality is achieved. Finally, students are exposed to some of the ideas underlying Rational-Emotive Therapy in a very self-meaningful way, which may generalize to their actual test-taking experience.

**DEMONSTRATION:** Students pair up and describe some of the thoughts they typically experience during an exam. After students have had some time to discuss this, the instructor generates some of the more frequently-occurring thoughts on an overhead transparency. As a group, the class then works to re-frame these thoughts so that they are more rational and less performance-crippling.

**MATERIALS:**
- One overhead transparency

**TIME:** Approximately 15 minutes

**PROCEDURES**:

1. Before beginning the material on Albert Ellis' Rational-Emotive Therapy, ask students to turn to someone sitting next to them. Ask students to close their eyes and imagine that they are getting ready to take an important exam for which they do not feel they are adequately prepared. Have students list some of the common thoughts that go through their minds under such conditions.

2. After students have had a chance to explore this, ask students to provide some examples from their lists. Place them on the transparency. Usually these take the form of, "I must do well on this test. I have to get a 100%. If I don't earn an "A", my life will be worthless. If I don't get a good grade on this test, my parents will kill me!," etc.

3. Describe Rational-Emotive Therapy for students. Explain that according to RET, people can become psychologically disordered due to the cognitive belief systems especially when one's beliefs are irrational and self-defeating. Ellis contends that those who suffer from depression are particularly likely to possess irrational beliefs (e.g., I must be perfect; I have to be the best mom; If I don't do x, my parents/spouse/boss will hate me; I'm a compete failure, etc.). These irrational beliefs often lead to feelings of depression, anxiety, and worthlessness. Through RET, the therapist challenges the client who holds these beliefs (e.g., how likely is that your mom/dad will hate you if you fail an exam?). The goal, of course, is for the client to begin to change his/her belief system and when falling prey to irrational beliefs to challenge these belief independently.

4. Have students re-frame the irrational beliefs on a transparency so that they represent more realistic thoughts.

5. Ask students if they find themselves engaging in re-framing when they experience these thoughts during an exam. Remind students that although some of them may experience test-anxiety, often this level of anxiety is confined to that particular situation. Ask students how it might feel if they experienced these thoughts across a wide variety of situations (e.g., work situations, family relations, spiritual matters, etc.) For those who suffer from major depression, irrational, self-defeating thoughts are likely to be chronic and pervasive—coloring many aspects of a person's world. Help students see the self-perpetuating nature of possessing such a belief structure. For those suffering from depression, such self-talk may prevent them from succeeding in a given situation, which just further reaffirms the person's already diminished self-concept.

**Related Readings:**

Eison, J. (1987). Using systematic desensitization and rational emotive therapy to treat test anxiety. In V. P. Makosky, L. G. Whittemore, and A. M. Rogers (Eds.), **Activities handbook for the teaching of psychology**, (Vol. **2**). Washington, DC: American Psychological Association.

Ellis, A. (1962). **Reason and emotion in psychotherapy.** New York: Lyle Stuart.

Ellis, A. (1993). Reflections on rational-emotive therapy. *Journal of Consulting and Clinical Psychology*, **61**, 199–201.

## Relaxation as a Treatment Strategy

The following activity provides students with the opportunity to learn an easy relaxation strategy. Tension and high levels of anxiety have been linked to a variety of psychological and physical disorders (e.g., hypertension, coronary heart disease, panic attacks, generalized anxiety disorders, phobias, etc.). Because of this, many treatment programs (e.g., stress management programs, therapy programs to alleviate panic attacks, phobic responses) incorporate relaxation and mental imagery components to help clients deal with stress and anxiety. The following activity walks students through a relaxation exercise. The activity helps students become aware of their own experience of tension and relaxation. A real plus is that instructors can tie this exercise into a variety of topics including health and stress issues, treatment options, physiological psychology, sport psychology, relaxation, and meditation as altered forms of consciousness, etc.

**DEMONSTRATION:** Students listen to a progressive relaxation script and monitor their own physiological experience.

**MATERIALS:**
■ Overhead Transparency (see OHT 19.2)

**TIME:**    Approximately 15 minutes

**PROCEDURES:**

1. This activity works well when discussing treatment options for the anxiety disorders (e.g., generalized anxiety disorder, obsessive-compulsive disorder, panic attacks, phobias, etc.).

2. The instructor might begin the activity by discussing some of the physical and psychological effects of tension and anxiety (e.g., irritability, depression, muscle tension, sleeping difficulties).

3. Announce to the class that they are going to engage in a kind of relaxation technique that is often used in treatment.

4. Tell students to put down their pencils, put their hands palms up on their desk, and to close their eyes. Tell students to try to tune out all other stimuli and to listen to your voice as you guide them toward feeling a greater sense of relaxation. Dim the lights.

5. Slowly, in a monotonous voice read through the relaxation script (see Relaxation Script on page 157 of this manual).

6. After you have finished, discuss with students their experiences. Do they feel more relaxed, warmer, more comfortable, a greater sense of peace? Ask the class if they use relaxation techniques like this in their own lives (e.g., to deal with text anxiety, before competing in an athletic event, etc.). Usually students talk about how they use variations of this technique to deal with very specific, high anxiety situations. Help students appreciate what people experience who suffer from high levels of anxiety on a chronic basis and how relaxation techniques can help the person change their thought patterns, their physiological health, etc.

7. Share with students some of the tips to become more proficient at relaxation via the prepared overhead (see **OHT 19.2**). Remind them that like most tasks, the more experience one has, the greater the level of proficiency.

**Related Readings:**

Bourne, E. J. (1995). **The anxiety and phobia workbook.** Oakland: New Harbinger Publications.

Jacobson, E. (1974). **Progressive Relaxation.** Chicago: University of Chicago Press.

# Relaxation Script

**Read the following script in a slow monotonous tone of voice:**

For the next several minutes, I would like you to concentrate your attention on your breathing. Try to get your breathing nice and even and regular (pause). Regular so that the same amount of time is taken breathing in (pause) as breathing out (pause). Nice, even, regular, rhythmic breathing (pause). If your mind wanders (pause) just gently and easily (pause) bring your attention back (pause) to your breathing (pause) noticing how even and regular (pause) your breathing is becoming. Nice, balanced, even breathing (pause).

As you are relaxing (pause) notice that sensation (pause) at the tip of your nose (pause) where the air feels slightly cooler when you breath in (pause) and slightly warmer when you breath out (pause). Allow your attention to focus on that sensation (pause) of coolness when you breath in (pause) and warmness when you breath out (pause 10 seconds).

You're feeling more relaxed and calm (pause). There's a comfortable, warm feeling on the top of your head (pause). The warm feeling is spreading downward (pause) across all sides of your head (pause). Warmth spreads down the back of your neck (pause), the sides of your head, and across your forehead (pause). You can feel the warmth spread across your eyebrows and eyelids (pause). Your forehead and eyelids are growing warm, relaxed, and heavy. The warmth spreads across your cheeks, your mouth, and into your chin (pause). Your whole face is growing pleasantly warmer and relaxed.

The warmth spreads into your neck and your shoulders (pause). Your neck and shoulders are growing heavy, relaxed, and warm (pause). The warmth spreads down (pause) into your upper arms (pause), into your forearms (pause), and into your hands (pause). Your arms and hands are growing heavy, relaxed, and warm.

The warmth spreads down (pause), down across your back (pause) and into the small of your back (pause). Your whole back area (pause) is growing pleasantly warm and relaxed.

The warmth spreads down (pause) across your chest (pause). Your breathing is (pause) comfortable, (pause) and relaxed (pause) and balanced. Nice even, balanced breathing.

The warmth spreads down (pause) across your stomach area (pause) and into your legs (pause). Your thighs (pause), your knees (pause), and your calves (pause) are growing heavier, more relaxed, warm (pause).

You can even feel the warmth spreading into your toes (pause). Your whole body (pause) is heavy (pause) and warm (pause) and relaxed (pause). The calmness even reaches your mind (pause). Your mind is at peace (pause), and your body is calm (pause). Your mind is at peace (pause) and your body is calm (10 second pause).

As you're relaxing, let yourself think of a pleasant and relaxing scene like a waterfall (ten second pause), a country lake (ten second pause), or a beautiful flower (ten second pause). Pick a scene (pause) and allow your mind (pause) to think about it for the next few minutes (ten second pause). What colors do you notice (ten second pause)? Are there any sounds (ten second pause)? Are there any other sensations (ten second pause)? The warmth of the sun (pause)? The feeling of a warm breeze (pause). Just let yourself stay with the scene (ten second pause).

As you're relaxing (pause) notice how your muscles feel (pause). Notice the comfortable sensations in your body (pause) of heaviness and warmth (pause). Some of you (pause) may even feel (pause) a comfortable tingling (ten second pause).

As you practice this exercise (pause) you might notice it (pause) getting easier and easier (pause). I'm going to count backwards (pause) from five to one (pause). When I get to one (pause) allow your eyes to open (pause). Five, feeling calm and relaxed (pause). Four, at peace with yourself (pause). Three, coming up (pause). Two, noticing sounds around you (pause). One, open your eyes.

---

# Tips For Effective Relaxation

1. Practice at least 20 minutes a day.

2. Find a quiet environment.

3. Practice at regular times.

4. Assume  a comfortable position.

5. Loosen any tight garments.

6. Decide not to worry about anything.

7. Assume a passive, detached attitude.

# Chapter 20

# Social Psychology

## Can We All Be
## Better Than Average?

**(Adapted from Bolt & Myers, 1983)**

The following activity illustrates the how the self-serving bias influences our perceptions of ourselves versus others.

**DEMONSTRATION:** Students complete an anonymous 4-item survey. Survey results are tabulated and presented during the next class meeting.

**MATERIALS:**
- A one-page handout for each student (see Handout 20.1)

**TIME:** Approximately 10 minutes

**PROCEDURES:**

1. One class period before discussing attribution and the self-serving bias, pass out the brief one-page survey to students (see **Handout 20.1**). Ask students to rate themselves in relation to the rest of the class on the four traits listed on the survey. Emphasize that the survey is anonymous and that they should NOT indicate their names. Collect the responses and tabulate for the next class period. Prepare a graph depicting the distribution of ratings on each dimension.

2. Since all of the traits should be normally distributed, it would be expected that the graph would show a normal distribution. However, this will not occur. The students will tend to rate themselves higher on the traits than they really are.

3. Point out to students that the average person in the class cannot be better than average—however, the results indicate that they are! Explain that most people have a tendency to see themselves more favorably than they see others. Suggest that our self-serving bias is not necessarily harmful. Lazarus (1979) suggested that such illusions

are necessary for our mental health. In fact, people who are depressed seem to be more accurate in their views of themselves than people who are not depressed.

**Related Readings:**

Bolt, M. and Myers, D. G. (1983). **Teacher's Resource and Test Manual to accompany Social Psychology,** New York: McGraw-Hill, Inc.

Lazarus, R. S. (1979). **Positive denial: The case for not facing reality. Psychology Today,** pp. 44–60.

# HOW DO YOU PERCEIVE YOURSELF?

Quickly and anonymously, guess where you stand on these traits relative to all the others in this class. On each line, fill in any number between 0 and 100.

1. My hunch is that about _____ % of the others in this class are more attractive than I am.

2. My hunch is that about _____ % of the others in this class are more ethical than I am.

3. My hunch is that about _____ % of the others in this class are more intelligent than I am.

4. My hunch is that about _____ % of the others in this class are more sympathetic than I am.

# The Positive Aspects
# of Conformity

The following activity illustrates how society expects people to conform to basic norms of conduct. Students are exposed to a student (a confederate) who does not seem to be conforming to basic class norms. This is a fun activity that students find pretty entertaining. We use it as a lecture starter for discussing conformity issues. Students usually attribute negative connotations to conforming behavior, forgetting that we all display conformity (the way we dress, the way we behave in certain situations—e.g., church, a funeral, a movie, a fast-food restaurant, etc.). This brief, vivid activity reminds students that an orderly society expects a certain level of conformity from its citizenry.

**DEMONSTRATION:** During lecture, a student confederate will engage in a series of behaviors that do not conform to class norms.

**MATERIALS:**
■ One extroverted student

**TIME:** Approximately 10 minutes

**PROCEDURES:**

1. Before class (outside of the classroom), enlist the help of an extroverted student. Explain that the class will be discussing conformity issues during the next class period and that you want to demonstrate how people react when others do not adhere to common norms for classroom behavior (e.g., remaining in ones' seat, keeping quiet, showing deference to the instructor, etc.)

2. Ask the student to wait for about five minutes for the class to settle down and then begin engaging in non-normative classroom behaviors. The behaviors should start out by being rather mild in nature and then gradually become more outrageous. For example, the confederate might:

   a)   make a comment out loud (Wow, that's really interesting!)
   b)   stand up and stretch
   c)   come to the front of the class and sit on the floor and continue to take notes
   d)   get up and turn on/off the lights
   e)   say in an obnoxious tone, "Is this really important ? Is it going to be on the test?"
   f)   run up and down the aisles of the classroom

3. Try not to react at first and continue lecturing. Students typically don't know how to react to this behavior—usually they try to ignore it at first, they begin giggling, but as the behavior continues, they can become irritated. We have had students tell the confederate to "shut up" or "knock it off".

4. After students begin reacting, ask them why they are irritated. Usually, students respond that the person is creating a disturbance, is being rude, doesn't know how to behave in a classroom, etc. Then after they have explored what they are feeling, ask them if anyone knows what the topic of lecture will be for the next class period. Usually someone remembers and you see a "eureka" effect come over students' faces.

5. Explain how you set them up with the help of a confederate and have the class give the confederate a big round of applause.

6. Lead the class in a discussion of conformity to social norms. Help the class explore some of the more beneficial aspects of obtaining a certain level of conformity in situations. What would society be like if we did not obtain citizenry conformity (e.g., if people did not conform to laws and routinely ran red lights? Did not wait their turn while standing in line at Wal-Mart?, etc.). How do we react when people do not adhere to basic social norms? You also might point out what happens when we travel to foreign countries and are unaware of the social norms—students who have traveled abroad can usually supply some examples of social gaffes they committed due to ignorance of cultural norms. The purpose of the discussion is to move students away from attaching only negative connotations to conforming behavior.

---

# The Kindness of Strangers: A Field Study in Helping

The following activity represents a field study in helping behavior. Students will have the opportunity to test their local communities helpfulness by employing the "lost letter technique." We find this activity to be a useful introduction to the material on helping behavior. It is an activity that students find involving. An added benefit to this activity is that students function as "mini experimenters" and have the opportunity to collect some data points, which is often difficult in a large section class.

**DEMONSTRATION:** Five students will write a brief message on a piece of paper and place the message in an envelope. Five students will each initialize a stamped, addressed envelope and drop their envelope in locations designated by the class. The class will then track which of the letters come back due to the "kindness of strangers."

**MATERIALS**:

- Five pieces of paper
- Five stamped, addressed envelopes
- Ten volunteers

**TIME**: Approximately 20 minutes

**PROCEDURES**:

1. Explain to the class that they are going to participate in a field study on helping behavior. Lead the class in a discussion of all the different reasons why we help others, e.g., being in a good mood, wanting to maintain our self-perceptions as a helpful person, because others have helped us (reciprocity norms), to look good in front of others (egoistic motives), etc. Then describe how the lost letter technique has been used by social psychologists as a creative method to unobtrusively assess helping behavior (e.g., to determine relative rates of helpfulness in rural vs. urban areas). Here the instructor can also talk about why such methods are particularly important in studying issues like helping behavior due to the influence of social desirability effect. Ask students what they would do if they found a lost letter that was addressed and had a stamp attached. Get a show of hands—would they post the letter, open it and read the letter, steal the stamps, walk on by, etc.

2. Show the class that you have addressed five envelopes to "resident" and included your home address (don't use your campus address . . . it can affect the level of helpfulness). Show the class that all of the letters have the appropriate postage affixed.

3. Solicit five volunteers from class to print a message on a sheet of paper to be enclosed in the envelope. Get the class involved in determining what message they want to convey if someone should open the envelope. Students often want to enclose a sarcastic message (e.g., you have been involved in an experiment on helping behavior and you failed!). We try to steer them toward more positive messages, e.g., "Have a nice day" and the like.

4. Solicit five other volunteers to drop the envelopes in various locations in the community. We usually have students drop some in spots around campus and others out in the community (e.g., the local shopping mall, a park, etc.). Depending on the area, an instructor also may attempt to replicate the "urban vs. rural" effect in the helping literature that suggests that one is more likely to receive help in rural areas as opposed to urban areas. If so, have students who will be in a large town or city drop some letters, while other students who come from more rural areas do the same thing. There are endless variations to this—placing the envelopes in areas frequented predominantly by males and females (e.g., rest rooms) and looking for gender effects in helpfulness.

5. Once the class has determined where the envelopes will be dropped, have each of the students who will be "doing the drop" initialize their envelope in small letters. In this way, the class can determine which letters have come back and from what locations.

6. This is an optional step but an instructor also may have members of the class predict which letters will be returned. After the experiment is over, they can check the accuracy of their predictions.

7. Have the volunteers drop the letters in the designated places. It is often helpful to do this activity on a Friday so that your volunteers have the weekend to perform the drop. This works quite well as many students tend to travel over the weekend (e.g., go home).

8. Each time a letter shows up in the mail, bring it to class and have the person who initialized the envelope verify their initials and remind the class where they dropped their letter.

9. After about two weeks, assess your data. What percentage of the letters came back? We usually get about a 60–80% response rate and use this information as an opportunity to remind the class that people are generally pretty helpful, particularly when they are not in danger and the costs of helping is relatively small. Sometimes we have received unexpected twists to this activity—when someone has opened the envelope, apparently read the message, sealed up the envelope, and posted it. In another case, someone opened the envelope and wrote a response on the enclosed sheet—"You have a nice day too" before posting it. This has lead to some interesting follow-up discussions with students regarding whether the person felt guilty about opening someone's mail, or whether the positive tone of our message prompted them to engage in helping behavior (i.e., mood effects, reciprocity of helping, etc.).

**Related Readings:**

Amato, P. R. (1983). Helping behavior in urban and rural environments: Field studies based on a taxonomic organization of helping episodes. *Journal of Personality and Social Psychology*, **66**, 571–586.

Levine, R. V., Martinez, T. S., Brase, G., & Sorenson, K. (1994). Helping in 36 U.S. cities. *Journal of Personality and Social Psychology*, **67**, 69–84

This activity illustrates how powerful the social situation is in determining individuals' behavior. Specifically, it shows that the presence of others can either facilitate or inhibit an individual's performance. When an individual performs a simple or well-learned task, the presence of an audience should improve performance (social facilitation). However, when the task is difficult or novel, the presence of an audience likely will inhibit or cause a decrement in performance (social inhibition). This demonstration is a modification of an exercise suggested by Cleary (1996).

**DEMONSTRATION:** Two volunteer students are asked to perform a task while two other students record their individual performance. The task that is performed requires a skill that one of the students has perfected and the other has not. Juggling, hacky-sac, hitting a wiffle ball, jumping rope are all tasks that usually work very well in a large classroom.

**MATERIALS:**
- Three soft juggling balls, hacky-sac ball, wiffle ball and plastic bat, or a jump rope
- Four student volunteers

**TIME:** Approximately 10–15 minutes

**PROCEDURES:**

1. Before lecturing on social influence, present this activity to the students who will find it involving and fun.

2. Choose one of the above listed activities. By a show of hands, ask students if they consider themselves to be good at performing this activity. Ask for one of these students to volunteer to demonstrate his or her skill. Then ask for another volunteer— someone who has never attempted the task or is very bad at it. Finally, ask for two more volunteers to act as the official time keepers.

3. Next, explain to the class that first we will be measuring each student's performance on the task outside of the classroom. Ask the volunteers to step out of the classroom and perform the task. Assign one of the other volunteers to each student to record his or her performance. For example, if the task is juggling, the recorder can count the number of minutes the student spends actually juggling vs. chasing dropped balls. After a few minutes, ask the students to re-enter the classroom and have the recorders report performance scores.

4. Now tell the volunteers that they will be performing the task in front of the class. Again have the recorders "officially" measure their performance. It's likely that the

student who has perfected the task will perform very well in front of the audience. In fact, they often improve over the first score. The student who is not good at the task usually shows a decrement in performance. The students and the class get into the activity and have a lot of fun.

5. Interview the two performers about how they felt performing the task in front of the audience. Use their responses to illustrate the concepts of social facilitation and inhibition.

**Related Reading:**

Cleary, R. J. (1996). Social Facilitation. *Instructor's Resource Manual to accompany Wade & Tavris Psychology* (4th Edition), Glenview: Addison Wesley Longman.

# Chapter 21

## Diversity

---

### Introducing Gender

**(Adapted from Bolt, 1999)**

---

Before students read a chapter on diversity or gender, have them complete this activity to focus on their perceptions of gender differences.

**DEMONSTRATION:** This activity involves asking students to complete a brief survey to identify their false stereotypes about gender.

**MATERIALS:**
- One sheet of notebook paper per student

**TIME:** Approximately 15 minutes

**PROCEDURES:**

1. Ask students to take out a piece of paper. Do **not** have them put their names on the paper.

2. Ask the class to consider whether or not men and women are different, other than anatomically. Tell them to draw the simple grid on the attached page (which should be made into an overhead transparency, see **OHT 2.1**) on their paper and give them the following instructions:

   "During the next few minutes I would like you to free-associate and write down everything you can think of when you see the words "Man" and "Woman." What you write should reflect your own feelings and **not** what you think others expect you to write. Think about all the men and women you know, as well as those you see on the streets, on television, or in magazines. Think about characteristics of each that you find pleasant and unpleasant."

3. Next, ask students to turn in their seats as best they can in the lecture hall and sort of group themselves into groups of 3 to 5.

4. Collect the anonymous papers with the help of a couple of "volunteers" and shuffle them and redistribute them such that no one has their own paper. After papers are redistributed, ask if anyone received their own paper back. If so, ask them to hand it over and trade it with another student in the class.

5. Encourage students to react informally to the lists. Ask them to consider whether or not the descriptions of both genders seem true. Remind students to make a clear case for their own position but at the same time be sensitive to the views of others.

6. After about 10 minutes, ask some male volunteers to read to the class the characteristics listed for "Man" while you put them on the overhead transparency. Then have several females do the same. Note descriptions that are repeated frequently for each sex.

7. Stimulate broader class discussion and lead into the lecture on gender by using the following questions:

   A. What do you think of the lists?
   B. Are we all responding differently? Similarly? Fairly? Accurately?
   C. Do any of the reactions surprise you?
   D. Do you think that gender differences are due to nature?     Nurture? Both?

**Related Reading:**

Bolt, M. (1999). Introducing gender. In **Instructor's Manual to accompany D. Myers' Social Psychology** (6th Edition). Boston: McGraw-Hill, Inc.

# Gender Differences

| Man | Woman |
|-----|-------|
|     |       |

# Gender Roles in the Home

**(Adapted from Doyle, 1985)**

During childhood, we acquire not only our gender identity but also many masculine or feminine behaviors and attitudes. Social learning theory in particular suggests that observation of adult models is crucial in this process. This activity asks students to reflect on the kinds of models of gender their parents were. If your students are of quite different ages, it may be interesting to compare the responses of the younger students with those of the older students. Are shifting gender roles apparent?

**DEMONSTRATION:** This activity involves asking students to complete a brief survey reflecting on the kinds of gender role models their parents were.

**MATERIALS:**
- One sheet of notebook paper per student

**TIME:** Approximately 5 minutes

**PROCEDURES:**

1.  Ask students to take out a piece of paper.

2.  Ask the class to complete the survey on the overhead transparency (see **OHT 21.2**).

3.  Discuss survey results based on course material on gender and social learning theory in terms of role models.

**Related Reading:**

Doyle, A. J. (1985). **Sex and gender: The human experience.** Boston: McGraw-Hill, Inc..

# Gender Roles in the Home: A Quiz

Father    Mother

1.  When you went out, who drove?
2.  Who fills out the income tax forms?
3.  Who writes the "Thank you" notes for the gifts received?
4.  Who is more likely to ask, "Where are my socks/stockings?"
5.  When the car needs repair, who takes it to the garage?
6.  Who does the laundry?
7.  Who dusts and vacuums?
8.  Who knows where to find the thermometer?
9.  Who knows where to find the pipe wrench?
10. Who knows where to find the summer clothes?
11. When you had guests for dinner, who made the drinks?
12. When you had guests for dinner, who made the coffee?
13. Who waters the house plants?
14. Who waters the lawn?
15. When you went on a trip, who packed the suitcases?
16. When you went on a trip, who packed the car?

The following activity illustrates many examples of memory construction and our tendency to assimilate events in a manner consistent with our pre-existing beliefs. The first student in each row is given a paragraph to read to the next person in the row. The second person then reports what they remember to the next person in the row and so on (similar to the old telephone game). The last person in the row is then asked to write down what they heard. The class then examines departures from the original paragraph. The instructor leads the class in a discussion of how oftentimes our memory distortions show reliable biases. According to research by Allport and Postman (1947), we often drop details form the story that do not fit our assumptions or cognitive categories (leveling). We also tend to stress details of the story that are congruent with our interpretations of how the event must have occurred (sharpening). Allport and Postman's research, for example, suggests that we may show a tendency to shift which person in the story was carrying the knife so that it appears in the African American's hand. This type of memory distortion is believed to occur because it seems more consistent with our stereotypes of whites and blacks for the black to be the assailant and to be acting in a threatening manner. We find this a useful way of introducing the subtle ways our cognitive processing can lead us to interpret events in a manner that confirms our pre-existing cognitive categorizations.

**DEMONSTRATION:** In rows, students verbally pass along a short story. After the story has passed through all the students, the class examines how the final stories departed from the original.

**MATERIALS:**
- One copy of the following paragraph for each row of students (see Handout 21.1)
- One sheet of notebook paper for the final student in each row

**TIME:** Approximately 20 minutes

**PROCEDURES:**

1. This activity works well to introduce the topic of confirmatory processing as a means of perpetuating our beliefs.

2. Have students stand up. Explain to the class that they will be playing the "telephone game" and that the first person in each row will be given a brief paragraph describing an incident.

3. The first person in the row should read the paragraph to the second person. The second person should then whisper what they think they heard to the third person and so on until all members of the row have been exposed to the story.

4. The person at the end of the row should be instructed to take out a sheet of paper and be prepared to write down the story as they have heard it.

5. After all rows have finished up, ask several students at the end of the rows to read their account of what they heard. This usually inspires a lot of laughing since no two stories are alike and most differ fairly dramatically.

6. Lead the class in a discussion of memory construction. Ask them to identify any examples of leveling or sharpening that they noted. Did the knife in the story end up with the African American? What about the briefcase? Is the knife now being brandished as a weapon rather than just being in the person's belt? What do these memory biases suggest to students about the way we encode and interpret information that is not consistent with our gender/racial stereotypes? How might such processes influence eyewitness testimony?

**Related Readings:**

Allport, G., & Postman, L. (1947). **The psychology of rumor.** New York: Henry Holt.

Bolt, M. (1999). Memory Construction. **In Instructor's Manual to accompany D. Myers' Social Psychology** (6th Edition). Boston: McGraw-Hill Inc.

A crowded city bus stopped
at Belmont Park at 9:00 A.M.
Among the passengers
were two males
who stood next to each other
toward the front of the bus.
One was a tall, well-dressed
African American
carrying a briefcase.
The other had a knife in his belt
and was shaking his left fist.

# Bibliography

Albrecht, K. (1980). **Brain Power.** Englewood Cliffs, NJ: Prentice-Hall.

Allport, G., & Postman, L. (1947). **The psychology of rumor.** New York: Henry Holt.

Amato, P. R. (1983). Helping behavior in urban and rural environments: Field studies based on a taxonomic organization of helping episodes. *Journal of Personality and Social Psychology*, **66**, 571–586.

Appleby, D. (1987). Producing a déjà vu experience. In **Activities Handbook for the teaching of psychology** (Vol. **2**). Washington, DC: American Psychological Association.

Atwater, E. and Duffy, K. G. (1999). **Psychology for Living** (6th Edition). Englewood Cliffs, NJ: Prentice-Hall.

Benjamin, L. T. (1991). Personalization and active learning in the large introductory psychology class. *Teaching of Psychology*, **18**, 68–74.

Bolt, M. (1999). Memory Construction. In **Instructor's Manual to accompany D. Myers' Social Psychology** (6th Edition). Boston: McGraw-Hill, Inc.

Bolt, M. (1999). Public and private self-consciousness. In **Instructor's Manual to accompany D. Myers' Social Psychology** (6th Edition). Boston: McGraw-Hill, Inc.

Bolt, M. and Myers, D. G. (1983). **Teacher's Resource and Test Manual to accompany Social Psychology.** Boston: McGraw-Hill, Inc.

Bourne, E. J. (1995). **The anxiety and phobia workbook.** Oakland: New Harbinger Publications.

Bugen, L. A. (1979). **Death and dying.** Dubuque, Iowa: Wm. C. Brown.

Carbone, E. (1998). **Teaching large classes: Tools and strategies.** Thousand Oaks, CA: Sage Publications, Inc.

Cauffman, E. (1999). **Instructor's Resource Manual with test questions to accompany Adolescence** (5th Edition). Boston: McGraw-Hill, Inc.

Ciccarelli, S. (1999). **Instructor's manual to accompany Feldman's Understanding Psychology** (5th Edition). Boston: McGraw-Hill, Inc.

Cleary R. J. (1996). Social Facilitation. **Instructor's Resource Manual to accompany Wade & Tavris Psychology** (4th Edition). Glenview: Addison Wesley Longman.

Coren, S., Ward, L. M., Ennis, J. T. (1999). **Sensation and perception** (5th Edition). Fort Worth: Harcourt Brace.

Craik, F. I., & Lockhart, R. S. (1972). Levels of processing: A framework for memory research. *Journal of Verbal Behavior*, **11**, 671–684.

Darwin, C. (1972/1965). **The expression of the emotions in man and animals.** Chicago: University of Chicago Press.

Deese, J. (1959). On the occurrence of particular verbal intrusions in immediate recall. *Journal of Experimental Psychology*, **58**, 17–22.

Diekhoff, G. M. (1987). The role of expectancies in the perception of language. In **Activities Handbook for the teaching of psychology** (Vol. **2**). Washington, DC: American Psychological Association .

Dollinger, S. J. (1998). The illusion of control. In **Activities handbook for the teaching of psychology** (Vol. **3**). Washington, DC: American Psychological Association.

Doyle, A. J. (1985). **Sex and gender: The human experience.** Boston: McGraw-Hill, Inc.

Eison, J. (1987). Using systematic desensitization and rational emotive therapy to treat test anxiety. In V. P. Makosky, L. G. Whittemore, and A. M. Rogers (Eds.), **Activities handbook for the teaching of psychology**, (Vol. **2**). Washington, DC: American Psychological Association.

Ekman, P. (1994). Strong evidence for universals in facial expressions: A reply to Russel's mistaken critique. *Psychological Bulletin*, **115**, 268–287.

Ekman, P. (1985). **Telling lies: Cues to deceit in the marketplace, politics and marriage.** New York: Norton.

Ekman, P., & Friesen, W. (1971). Constants across cultures in the face and emotion. *Journal of Personality and Social Psychology*, **17**, 124–129.

Fisher, J. (1979). **Body Magic**. New York: Stein & Day Publishers.

Ellis, A. (1993). Reflections on rational-emotive therapy. *Journal of Consulting and Clinical Psychology*, **61**, 199–201.

Ellis, A. (1962). **Reason and emotion in psychotherapy.** New York: Lyle Stuart.

Gardner, H. (1983). **Frames of mind: The theory of multiple intelligences.** New York: Basic Books.

Greene, J. O., O'Hair, H.D., Cody, M. J., & Yen, C. (1985). Planning and control of behavior during deception. *Human Communication Research*, **11**, 335–364.

Hilgard, E. R. (1965). **Hypnotic suggestibility.** New York: Harcourt Brace.

Harper, G. F. (1979). Introducing Piagetian concepts through the use of familiar and novel illustrations. *Teaching of Psychology*, **6** (1), 58–59.

Hass, R. (1984). Perspective taking and self-awareness. *Journal of Personality and Social Psychology*, **46**, 788–798.

Hyde, T. S. & Jenkins, J. J. (1973). Recall of words as a function of semantic, graphic, and syntactic orienting tasks. *Journal of Verbal Learning and Verbal Behavior*, **12**, 471–480.

Izard, C. E. (1977). <u>**Human emotions.**</u> New York: Plenum.

Jacobson, E. (1974). **Progressive Relaxation**. Chicago: University of Chicago Press.

Johnson, G. B. (1966). Penis envy or pencil needing? *Psychological Reports,* **19**, 758.

Kahneman, D., & Tversky, A. (1973). On the psychology of prediction. *Psychological Review*, **80**, 237–251.

Kemble, E. D., Filipi, T., & Gravlin, L. (1985). Some simple classroom experiments on cerebral lateralization. *Teaching of Psychology*, **12**, 81–83.

Kobasa, S. C. (1979). Stressful life events, personality, and health: An inquiry into hardiness. *Journal of Personality and Social Psychology*, **37**, 1–11.

Kunz, J. R. M. & Finkel, A. J. (Eds.) (1987). **The American Medical Association Family Medical Guide** by the American Medical Association. New York: Random House.

Langer, E. J. (1975). The illusion of control. *Journal of Personality and Social Psychology*, **32**, 311–328.

Lazarus, R. S. (1979). Positive denial: The case for not facing reality. *Psychology Today,* pp. 44–60.

Levine, R. V., Martinez, T. S., Brase, G., & Sorenson, K. (1994). Helping in 36 U.S. cities. *Journal of Personality and Social Psychology*, **67**, 69–84.

Loftus, E. F., & Palmer, J. C. (1974). Reconstruction of automobile destruction: An example of the interaction between language and memory. *Journal of Verbal Learning and Verbal Behavior*, **13**, 585–589.

MacLeod, C. M. (1991). Half a century of research on the Stroop effect: An integrative review. *Psychological Bulletin*, **109**, 163–203.

Miller, G. A. (1956). The magical number seven, plus or minus two: Some limits on our capacity for processing information. *Psychology Review*, **63**, 81–97.

Miller, G. A., & Isard, S. (1963). Some perceptual consequences of linguistic rules. *Journal of Verbal Learning and Verbal Behavior*, **2**, 217–228.

Modell, H. I. (Ed) and Michael, J. A. (Ed) (1993). **Promoting active learning in the life science classroom.** New York: New York Academy of Sciences.

Nickerson, R. S., & Adams, M. J. (1979). Long-term memory for a common object. *Cognitive Psychology*, **11**, 287–307.

Nyquist, J. D., Wulff, D. H., and Abbott, R. D. (1997). Students' perceptions of large classes. In M. Weimer (Ed.), **New directions for teaching and learning: Teaching large classes well** (pages 17–30). San Francisco: Jossey-Bass.

Rosenthal, R., & Jacobson, L. (1968). **Pygmalion in the classroom.** New York: Holt, Rinehart & Winston.

Rozin, P., and Jonides, J. (1977). Mass reaction time measurement of the speed of the nerve impulse and the duration of mental processes in class. *Teaching of Psychology*, **4**(2), 91–94.

Silberman, M. (1996). **Active learning: 101 strategies to teach any subject.** Needham Heights, MA: Allyn and Bacon.

Singer, J., and Switzer, E. (1980). **Mind-Play.** Englewood Cliffs, NJ: Prentice-Hall.

Stroop, J. R. (1935). Studies of interference in serial verbal reactions. *Journal of Experimental Psychology*, **18**, 643–662.

Watson, D. (1990). A neat little demonstration of the benefits of random assignment of subjects in an experiment. In V. P. Makosky, C. C. Sileo, L. G. Whittemore, C. P. Landry, & M. L. Skutley (Eds.) **Activities handbook for the teaching of psychology:** Vol. 3 (p. 4). Washington, DC: American Psychological Association.

Whittemore, C. P. Landry, & M. L. Skutley (Eds.) **Activities handbook for the teaching of psychology:** Vol. 3 (p.4). Washington, DC: American Psychological Association.

Whitford, F. (1996). Teaching psychology (2nd Edition). **A guide for the new instructor.** Englewood Cliffs, New Jersey: Prentice-Hall.

Zakrajsek, T. (1997). **Instructor's Manual to accompany Feldman's Understanding Psychology** (4th Edition). Boston: McGraw-Hill, Inc.

**About the Authors**

Patricia A. Jarvis, Ph.D., is a Professor of Psychology at Illinois State University in Normal, Illinois. She received her Ph.D. in Experimental Psychology with an emphasis in Developmental Psychology in 1986 from Virginia Commonwealth University. She has authored five supplementary manuals for college-level instructors. In addition, she has made numerous presentations on teaching at Illinois State University and at regional and national conferences. She regularly teaches large ($N < 300$) sections of Introductory Psychology. She has received national and college-level awards for her teaching excellence at SUNY Plattsburgh and at Illinois State University.

Cynthia R. Nordstrom, Ph.D., is an Assistant Professor of Psychology at Illinois State University in Normal, Illinois. She received her Ph.D. in Industrial/Organizational Psychology in 1991 from the University of Akron. She has made numerous presentations on teaching at Illinois State University and routinely teaches large ($N > 300$) sections of Introductory Psychology. She has received awards for her teaching excellence from Illinois State University.

Karen B. Williams, Ph.D., is an Associate Professor of Psychology at Illinois State University in Normal, Illinois. She received her Ph.D. in Industrial/Organizational Psychology in 1985 from Iowa State University. She has made numerous presentations on teaching at Illinois State University and routinely teaches large ($N > 300$) sections of Introductory Psychology. She has been recognized for her teaching excellence at Illinois State University.

**Chapter 2**
*Reflections, Thoughts and Advice on Teching Introductory Psychology:* "Reflections, Thoughts and Advice on Teching Introductory Psychology" by Paul Rosenfeld. Reprinted by Zakrajsek (1996) in the Instructors Manual to Accompany Feldman's Understanding Psychology (4/e).
*Tips for Effective Management of Large Sections:* TEACHING PSYCHOLOGY: A GUIDE FOR THE NEW INSTRUCTOR by Whitford, ©1996, Adapted by permission of Prentice-Hall, Inc., Upper Saddle River, NJ.

**Chapter 5**
*Random Assignment:* Usefulness and Limitations: "The Benefits of Random Assignment of Subjects in an Experiment" by David L. Watson in Makosky, Sileo, Whittemore, Landry and Skutley (Eds.), Activities Handbook for the Teaching of Psychology, Vol. 3, 3-4. Copyright © 1990 by the American Psychological Association. Adapted with permission.

**Chapter 6**
*Reaction-Time Measure of Neural Transmission and Mental Processes:* "Reaction-Time Measure of Neural Transmission and Mental Processes" from Instructor's Resources for use with Myers Psychology 2/e. pp.2-3 (1989) Worth. Adapted with permission.

**Chapter 7**
*Demonstrating Binocular Vision:* Fisher, J. (1979) Body Magic. Briarcliff Manor, NY: Stein and Day. pp. 39-40 Adapted with permission.
*Sound Location:* Fisher, J. (1979) Body Magic. Briarcliff Manor, NY: Stein and Day. p. 50, 113-114 Adapted with permission.
*Understanding Weber's Law:* From Coren, Ward, and Enn's Sensation and Perception (5th Edition) 1999. Adapted with permission.

**Chapter 8**
*Dream Interpretation:* Reprinted with the permission of Simon & Schuster from MIND-PLAY: THE CREATIVE USES OF FANTASY by Jerome L. Singer and Ellen Switzer, Copyright © 1980 by Jerome L. Singer and Ellen Switzer.
*Where Did I hear that Before? Creating a Déjà Vu Experience:* "Producing A Déjà Vu Experience" by Drew Appleby in Makosky, Sileo, Whittemore, Landry and Skutley (Eds.), Activities Handbook for the Teaching of Psychology, Vol. 2, 78-79. Copyright © 1987 by the American Psychological Association. Adapted with permission.

**Chapter 10**
*Recall a Penny:* "Long-Term Memory for a Common Object" by Raymond S. Nickerson and Marilyn Jager Adams in Cognitive Psychology Volume 11, 287-307 (1979). Reprinted with permission.
*Demonstrating Levels-of-Processing Theory:* "Demonstrating Levels-of-Processing Theory" by Zakrajsek (1996) in the Instructors Manual to accompany Feldman's Understanding Psychology (4/e).

**Chapter 11**
*The Importance of Expectancies in Understanding Languages:* "The Role of Expectancies in the Perception of Language" by George M. Diekhoff in Makosky, Sileo, Whittemore, Landry and Skutley (Eds.), Activities Handbook for the Teaching of Psychology, Vol. 2, 57-59. Copyright © 1987 by the American Psychological Association. Adapted with permission.

**Chapter 13**
*The Facial Feedback Hypothesis:* by Bolt and Myers (1983) in the Teacher's Resource Manual to Accompany Social Psychology.

**Chapter 14**
*Assimilation and Accommodation:* "Assimilation and Accommodation" by G. Harper in Teaching of Psychology, 1979. Reprinted by permission of Lawrence Erlbaum.
*Adolescent Sexuality:* "Penis and Vagina Activity" by E. Cauffman (1999) in the Instructor's Resource Manual with Test Questions to Accompany Adolescence (5/e).

**Chapter 15**
*Who Am I?:* "Who Am I?" by L. Bugen (1979) in Death and Dying (originally published by William C. Brown Publishers).
*How Much Do You Know About Aging?:* Psychology for Living 6/e by Atwater/Duffy. ©1998 Reprinted by Permission of Prentice-Hall, Inc., Upper Saddle River, NJ.

**Chapter 16**
*A Covert Test of Public Self-Consciousness:* "Public and private self-consciousness" by M. Bolt (1999) in the Instructor's Manual to Accompany Myers' Social Psychology.

**Chapter 17**
*How Hardy Are You?:* "Stress and Health: How Hardy are You?" by Suzanne C. Ouellette. Reprinted by permission of author.
*The Powerful Need to Control:* "The Illusion of Control" by Stephen J. Dollinger, in Makosky, Sileo, Whittemore, Landry and Skutley (Eds.), Activities Handbook for the Teaching of Psychology, Vol. 3, 170-171. Copyright © 1990 by the American Psychological Association. Adapted with permission.

**Chapter 18**
*Misconceptions About Mental Disorders:* PSYCHOLOGY 4/E I/R/M by Cleary (Wade/Tavris), ©1990. Adapted with permission of Prentice-Hall, Inc., Upper Saddle River, NJ.
*Learned Helplessness:* "Learned Helplessness" by E. Cauffman (1999) in the Instructor's Resource Manual with Test Questions to Accompany Adolescence (5/e).

**Chapter 19**
*Ethical Issues Pertaining to Therapy:* "Some ethical issues pertaining to therapy" by S. Ciccarelli (1999) in the Instructor's Manual to Accompany Feldman's Understanding Psychology (5/e).
*Exploring Rational-Emotive Therapy Through Irrational Beliefs:* "Using Systematic Desensitization and Rational Emotive Therapy to Treat Test Anxiety" in Makosky, Sileo, Whittemore, Landry and Skutley (Eds.), Activities Handbook for the Teaching of Psychology, Vol. 2, 159-161. Copyright © 1987 by the American Psychological Association. Adapted with permission.

**Chapter 20**
*Can We All be Better than Average?:* by Bolt and Myers (1983) in the Teacher's Resource Manual to Accompany Social Psychology.
*Social Facilitation & Inhibition:* PSYCHOLOGY 4/E I/R/M by Cleary (Wade/Tavris), ©1990. Adapted with permission of Prentice-Hall, Inc., Upper Saddle River, NJ.

**Chapter 21**
*Introducing Gender:* by Bolt (1999) in the Instructor's Manual to Accompany Social Psychology.
*Gender Roles in the Home:* by A. Doyle (1985) in Sex and Gender: The Human Experience. Wm. C. Brown.
*Race Stereotyping in Memory Construction:* by Bolt (1999) in the Instructor's Manual to Accompany Myers' Social Psychology.